GENEALOGIST'S GUIDE TO
GETTING ORGANIZED

---

familytree

Dublin, NH

Portions of this book were previously published in *Family Tree Magazine*. Find more resources at <www.familytreemagazine.com>.

ISBN: 978-1-961793-79-8

contents

Editor **Andrew Koch**

Art Director and Cover Designer **Julie Barnett**

Digital Editor **Melina Papadopoulos**

New Media Editor **Rachel Christian**

eLearning Producer **Amanda Epperson**

Contributing Editors **Lisa A. Alzo, Rick Crume, David A. Fryxell, Nancy Hendrickson, Sunny Jane Morton, Maureen A. Taylor**

Additional Designers **Lori Pedrick, Katharine van Itallie**

VP Production and New Media **Paul Belliveau, Jr.**

Production Director **Dave Ziarnowski**

Production Manager **Brian Johnson**

Senior Production Artists **Jenn Freeman, Rachel Kipka**

Senior Ad Production Coordinator **Janet Selle**

New Media Designer **Amy O'Brien**

Digital Marketing Specialists **Jessica Garcia, Holly Sanderson**

Email Marketing Specialist **Eric Bailey**

eCommerce Manager **Alan Henning**

VP Consumer Marketing **Brook Holmberg**

VP Single Copy Sales **Sherin Pierce**

EDITORIAL OFFICES:
PO Box 520, 1121 Main Street, Dublin, NH 03444
familytree@yankeepub.com

Family Tree Magazine, published in the United States,
is not affiliated with the British *Family Tree Magazine*,
with Family Tree Maker software or with Family Tree DNA.

FAMILY TREE MAGAZINE IS A DIVISION OF
YANKEE PUBLISHING, INC:
President and CEO **Jamie Trowbridge**

Vice Presidents **Paul Belliveau, Jr., Ernesto Burden, Judson D. Hale Jr., Brook Holmberg, Jennie Meister, Sherin Pierce**

TOP SECRETS

Professional genealogists share their 12 top tips for staying organized, catching every clue, and making the most of your research minutes.

by JANINE ADAMS

Genealogy researchers love the thrill of the hunt. When you're on the prowl for old records, it's hard to match that feeling of triumph when you finally net the will or deed you're after. Perhaps less thrilling, though, is the need to organize all the information you find. But unless you do, that information will be less useful to you or the generations that follow. As a professional organizer and an avid genealogist, I've found that organizing my research time can make my research sessions more successful and enjoyable.

Getting your research organized isn't optional if you're serious about discovering your family tree. You can bet that professional genealogists, who might trace the family trees of three or four or 10 clients at a time, have devised clever ways to organize information and maximize their research time. There's much to learn from these pros. Four of these experts divulged their top organization principles to me—and I'm sharing them so you, too, can find your family faster.

1

KNOW YOUR RESEARCH QUESTION.

Start each research session knowing what you're looking for. "Have a very specific research question in front of you so you can keep focused on it," says Drew Smith, author of the book *Organize Your Genealogy* (Family Tree Books) and podcaster at the Genealogy Guys Podcast <genealogyguys.com>. An example might be, "Where was my great-grandmother buried?" Narrowing the focus of a session to an individual, or possibly a couple, can help you avoid distractions and keep you from feeling overwhelmed as you search online databases and consider which record might belong to your family.

D. Joshua Taylor, president of the New York Geographical and Biographical Society <www.newyorkfamily history.org> and a host of PBS's "Genealogy Roadshow," limits his personal research to two or three projects—that is, questions needing answered—at a given time. "I try to be very diligent about not shifting my focus, but it's much easier said than done," he says. He finds that making the conscious decision to explore only a few specific questions keeps his focus on resources that may pertain to these questions, boosting his productivity.

Taylor sets a time limit of three to six months to finish a research project. If he hasn't found the answer he seeks by the deadline, he puts the project on the back burner and moves on to another question. He keeps a list of his projects, so he always knows which one will come into the rotation when he finishes or tables the current project. "I actually have the next two years of research mapped out."

2

BE REALISTIC ABOUT WHAT YOU CAN GET DONE.

When you're creating a plan for your research session, set yourself up for success by being realistic about what you can accomplish in the time you're able to spend. (This is good advice for organizing any aspect of your life, by the way.) This helps you avoid having to stop midstream. "I try to imagine how long it will take me to do a project, and it helps me plan what I want to accomplish," Taylor says.

There's no need to set aside a whole day to research, Smith adds. He says that for most people, two hours of research is probably the maximum before they feel mentally drained. And short sessions are much easier to fit into your busy schedule. I research every morning for about 30 minutes. My to-do list is brief for these bite-sized sessions, and they're usually productive. For more-involved research questions, I add longer sessions about once a month.

3

JOT DOWN YOUR "BRIGHT SHINY OBJECTS" FOR LATER.

You undoubtedly know the temptation of coming across unexpected information on a family member you weren't researching. These BSOs (Bright Shiny Objects) can distract you from the question you started off with. It's human nature to want to explore an unanticipated find. To stay focused on your research question, Smith suggests taking a moment to bookmark or write down the BSO so you can come back to it later. "Make a note for yourself so you won't have that [distraction] running around in your head," Smith says.

Taylor tries to anticipate distractions, deciding before starting a session what he is and isn't going to research. "I'm never as efficient when I'm going in a million different directions when I'm researching," he says. "So I try to stay focused on the research I set out to do." He keeps a log called Other People, where he notes information that doesn't fall into his current research plan but merits further investigation in the future.

tip Organization tools with tagging or labeling systems, like Evernote <www.evernote.com> and Trello <trello.com>, let you tag information with ancestors' names, dates, places, file types, subjects and more. This cross-references your information and makes it easy to retrieve all the notes assigned to the tag you search for.

A research log lets you jump right into a task instead of spending the first 10 minutes figuring out where you left off, and keeps you from duplicating efforts.

4 KEEP A RESEARCH LOG.

A research log lets you maximize your research time by helping you jump right into a task, instead of spending the first 10 minutes figuring out where you left off. It also stops you from duplicating efforts. "To me, it's like Hansel and Gretel with a breadcrumb trail, except the birds are not going to pick up those breadcrumbs," says Thomas MacEntee, the genealogist behind GenealogyBargains <www.genealogybargains.com>. It's up to you to search out and keep track of these clues.

Your research log might be a spreadsheet or a list in your genealogy software where you record pertinent information: the date of your research, ancestors searched, records you used, what you found, information extracted from that source, and resources you need to consult next. For example, if you discovered a name in an online index and you need to request a copy of the record or find it on microfilm, record these tasks in your research log. MacEntee suggests checking out different research log formats and trying the one that feels best to you. "You've got to find the method that works best for your habits," MacEntee says. "Otherwise you're not going to stay with it."

I keep a freeform log in Evernote <www.evernote.com>, with one note per research session that I file in an annual research log notebook. It doesn't get much simpler than that. After a number of failed attempts at more complicated logs, this simple system has allowed me to create the habit of recording what I did and what my next steps are.

While searching for your ideal system, keep data portability in mind. You want to be able to download or export your data, so you can back it up, create a report with it, or import it into a new system if needed.

5 RECORD NEGATIVE FINDINGS.

Of course you record the information you find in your research. But taking note of what you *didn't* find can be very helpful as well, Smith says. This can help you avoid checking the same sources again. Paying attention to negative results also can provide valuable clues.

"*Not* finding something can tell you just about as much as finding something," Smith says. For example, if someone doesn't show up as expected in a census or city directory, you might have an indication he or she moved away or has died. Look for him in death records and in records of other places (such as where other relatives have moved).

6 USE YOUR RESEARCH LOG AS A PLACE TO HOLD UNPROVEN DISCOVERIES.

It can be challenging to keep track of finds that may or may not be legitimate—theories about where your ancestor may have migrated or how a same-surname family is related to yours. You don't want to prematurely give them credence, but you also don't want to lose track of the clue. Your research log is the perfect place to record this unproven information, suggests MacEntee, who calls this his "sandbox." It's a holding place where you can explore the clues more until you prove or disprove them.

It's safer to store these clues in your log rather than in your genealogy software or family tree. "Nothing goes into my genealogy database until I've proven it through the research log," MacEntee says. That way, your database contains only sourced facts and you can feel good about sharing your tree with others.

SAMPLE GENEALOGY WORKFLOW

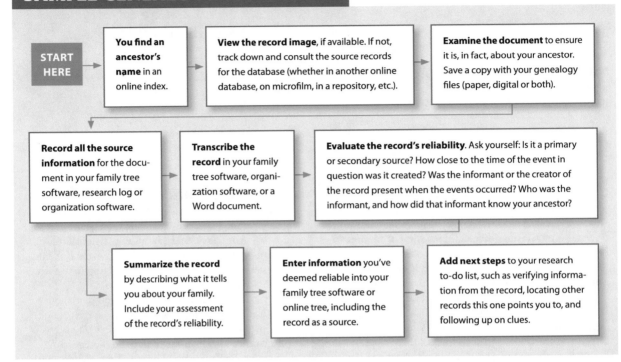

START HERE → **You find an ancestor's name** in an online index. → **View the record image**, if available. If not, track down and consult the source records for the database (whether in another online database, on microfilm, in a repository, etc.). → **Examine the document** to ensure it is, in fact, about your ancestor. Save a copy with your genealogy files (paper, digital or both).

Record all the source information for the document in your family tree software, research log or organization software. → **Transcribe the record** in your family tree software, organization software, or a Word document. → **Evaluate the record's reliability**. Ask yourself: Is it a primary or secondary source? How close to the time of the event in question was it created? Was the informant or the creator of the record present when the events occurred? Who was the informant, and how did that informant know your ancestor?

Summarize the record by describing what it tells you about your family. Include your assessment of the record's reliability. → **Enter information** you've deemed reliable into your family tree software or online tree, including the record as a source. → **Add next steps** to your research to-do list, such as verifying information from the record, locating other records this one points you to, and following up on clues.

7 USE RESEARCH CHECKLISTS.

Creating a workflow—a step-by-step process for doing research and working with your results—can help you keep your research sessions focused and efficient. "You might even want to use a flowchart that gives you all the steps," Smith says. You can use our sample workflow (above) or create your own that's customized to your research.

Smith suggests creating checklist templates in a word processing document, spreadsheet software, note-taking app (such as Evernote), or another program of your choice. Copy and then individualize your checklists as needed for each project or research session. These checklists can help you make the most of the records you discover and mine every last clue. Consider using the following kinds of research checklists, and add others you find helpful:
- Your research workflow
- US and state censuses that occurred during the lifetime of the person you're researching
- Sources you plan to consult on a library visit
- Source information to note for each record you find
- Spelling variants of your ancestors' names
- Research log to record your findings and source citations (see tip No. 4)
- Books you own (to avoid duplicate purchases)

8 KEEP TRACK OF NEXT STEPS.

Make a note of where you left off at the end of every session. Then when you sit down to research next time, you can simply consult that note and see what's next. I write down my next steps in my research log at the end of each session, and it's been an invaluable time-saving habit.

MacEntee describes these notations as "a to-do list with a little more flavor to it." "So many of us get 15 minutes in an evening to research, and then we put it down and come back a week later," he says. "Writing down where you left off cuts down on duplication of effort."

Taylor organizes his research task lists by repository, which might be a library or an online database. Then when he goes to the Family History Library <www.familysearch.org> or Ancestry <ancestry.com>, he can do all his lookups, even if they're not related to a current research project.

9 KEEP YOUR ORGANIZATION TOOLS SIMPLE AND CONSISTENT.

The simpler the system, the easier it is to follow. "Start simple," Smith advises. "Once you have that mastered, you can add complexity, like color coding, if you want. But I think for most researchers, the simpler the better."

In working with my organization clients, I've found that complicated techniques requiring things like cross-referencing and special labels might be attractive, but they can be time-intensive to follow—so you won't do it. It's far better to establish an easy system that you have a fighting chance of following. I've tried and failed to keep complex research logs, filling out fields for where, when and what I found. I needed something simpler. When I finally started allowing myself to create a note in Evernote and write about each session freeform, I was able to create the habit of logging all my searches.

MacEntee suggests creating a digital file-naming system that makes it easy to identify the file by person or date. He also recommends descriptive file names so you know what's in a file without having to open it. Name your files with a consistent scheme. Mine is Year-Document Type-Person-Locality, as in: *1938-death certificate-GW Adams-Indianapolis IN.jpg*. Starting each file name with a year makes the files line up chronologically in the folders on my hard drive. You might want them in alphabetical order by surname, or some other arrangement.

10 DO WHAT WORKS FOR YOU.

The best way to organize your research is the way that works for you, which is why Taylor urges you to personalize any organizational system you try. "Don't try and take something off the shelf and assume that every aspect will apply to your research," he says. Instead, take what you learn in a lecture or an article (even this article!) and customize it for your own needs, rather than trying to replicate it.

But do consider others who might one day need to sort through your research, adds Denise Levenick, blogger at The Family Curator <www.thefamilycurator.com> and author of *How to Archive Family Keepsakes*. A good system will be open and accessible to your heirs, who may need to determine what information goes with what person, and what's important to keep.

People have a tendency to give up on trying to get organized the moment it starts to feel like it isn't working. But instead of jumping to another strategy, or just deciding organizing your research isn't worth the effort, tweak your techniques. Think about what is and isn't working for you, and write it down. Can you alter the parts that aren't working to be more like the parts that are? Often, simplifying a system by just removing the steps you're resisting is enough of a modification to make it work. If you love color-coding file names, research log entries and paper folders, and you'll do it consistently, great. If not, it can be an impediment. In that case, just leave out the color-coding step.

11 DON'T RUSH.

I always urge my organizing clients to give a new system time before deciding it's not for them. Creating an organizing system that works requires creating new habits. And new habits take time to establish.

"Genealogy isn't a sprint, it's a marathon," MacEntee says. "You want to set yourself up to win that marathon in the long run." That means there's no need to cut corners. It also means that patience is a virtue.

Researching your family tree is not something you do in a week or a year. Taking time to organize your findings is just part of that process. The same holds true for inherited family archives. Levenick suggests taking your time when you're working with a family archive, to get to know what's in it. Carefully go through the photos and the letters and see what you have, trying not to disrupt the groups or order of items.

She's found that spending time with her family photos has helped her in her genealogy research. For example, she recognized a name on the family tree of a DNA match because that name appeared on an old photo. If she'd rushed through her photos, rather than carefully examining them, she might not have made this connection.

12 BE KIND TO YOURSELF.

It's unrealistic to expect that you'll to be able to organize all your information or your entire family archive in a week, says Levenick. And you may not have access to all the resources, like archival quality storage materials or a flatbed scanner, that you'd like. Be kind to yourself. "You just have to do the best you can with the funds and knowledge you have," she says. "And that's okay."

Don't beat yourself up if an organizing system you read about or heard an expert talk about isn't working for you. It doesn't mean there's something wrong with you. "We're all unique," Taylor says, "and genealogy is part creativity."

Organizing your genealogy information takes time. But it's time well spent. Investing that time up front in setting up a research log, workflow or staying-focused strategies will pay off down the road in more genealogy finds. You'll save hours and effort locating information and documents.

Honestly, wouldn't you rather spend more time researching and less time looking for things? As MacEntee says, "We should be looking for ancestors, we shouldn't be looking for stuff." •

Janine Adams, a certified professional organizer and author of the Organize Your Family History blog <www.organizeyourfamilyhistory.com>, applies the organizing strategies she uses with clients every day to her own genealogy research.

GENEALOGY PROJECT MANAGEMENT WORKSHEET

PROJECT 1:	PROJECT 2:	PROJECT 3:
Sub-project 1:	**Sub-project 1:**	**Sub-project 1:**
To-do list	To-do list	To-do list
1.	1.	1.
2.	2.	2.
3.	3.	3.
4.	4.	4.
5.	5.	5.
Sub-project 2:	**Sub-project 2:**	**Sub-project 2:**
To-do list	To-do list	To-do list
1.	1.	1.
2.	2.	2.
3.	3.	3.
4.	4.	4.
5.	5.	5.
Sub-project 3:	**Sub-project 3:**	**Sub-project 3:**
To-do list	To-do list	To-do list
1.	1.	1.
2.	2.	2.
3.	3.	3.
4.	4.	4.
5.	5.	5.
Sub-Project 4:	**Sub-Project 4:**	**Sub-Project 4:**
To-do list	To-do list	To-do list
1.	1.	1.
2.	2.	2.
3.	3.	3.
4.	4.	4.
5.	5.	5.
Weekly review dates	Weekly review dates	Weekly review dates
Monthly review dates	Monthly review dates	Monthly review dates
Annual review dates	Annual review dates	Annual review dates

habits
to make

Your genealogy life will be more organized and efficient when you make these 17 habits part of your research routine.

BY DANA MCCULLOUGH

❧ **WITH THE NEW** year comes a list of resolutions. Whether or not you make (and keep) resolutions, now is a great time to plan what you want to do differently or better in the coming year. It's easy for genealogists to get bogged down in all the information they take in: dates and names, piles of paper, digitized documents, unlabeled old photos, an overflowing email inbox, countless email notifications of potential matches in genealogy websites and hundreds (maybe even thousands, for some of you shutter-happy folks) of new digital photos taken on your smartphone each year.

Don't spend another year feeling like you barely have a handle on your research. Instead, start this year with these habits that will make it easier to organize your research, maintain your files and keep up with what's new in the genealogy world. Instead, follow our 17 tips to make you a better genealogy researcher in the next year.

1 Research regularly.

For many of us, it's difficult to find the time to regularly do genealogy research. Work, family and other responsibilities usually take priority.

Instead of waiting until you have the time to do genealogy, make sure you'll have time by scheduling a session each week or month to enjoy the hobby you love. For example, you could make the last Saturday of the month your "genealogy day." Go to the library or search online for the morning, afternoon, evening or all day—whatever fits into your busy life.

2 Cite your sources.

When you start genealogy research, you may think it's unnecessary to document the source of each family fact. But the more research you do, the more you realize it's easy to lose track of where you learned what—and it's important to be able to retrace your research steps.

On some genealogy websites, you can save source documents for later reference to a general "shoebox" (on Ancestry.com <ancestry.com>) or "source box" (on FamilySearch <www.familysearch.org>). You also can cite sources for individuals in your online tree by attaching records to their personal profiles. On FamilySearch, you can save sources from other websites (URLs as well as images or other media) with the Tree Source bookmarklet tool <www.recordseek.com>. Remember to download an image of each historical record you find online, so you'll still have a copy even if you don't have online access to that site in the future.

Most family tree software has built-in tools to help you fully document your sources, too. If you're not sure how to cite sources, consult *Evidence Explained: Citing History Sources from Artifacts to Cyberspace* by Elizabeth Shown Mills (Genealogical Publishing Co.) and download our free source citation cheat sheet at <familytreemagazine.com/info/genealogyessentials>.

3 Schedule time to organize.

After my daughter was born in 2015, my husband and I took what seemed like hundreds of new digital photos every month to document her first year. Having the photos is great, but it's also overwhelming to keep up with organizing them. I began setting aside about 15 minutes each week to sort through photos, identify the best ones and rename them so we can easily find them when working on photo projects.

Digitized and paper genealogy documents and old family photos can pile up just as quickly as the photos and videos you take on your smartphone. Make time regularly to rename and sort your saved records, using a consistent file naming and organization system. If you don't yet have an organization system, choose one that works for you. Setting it up may take an initial investment of your energy, but in the long run you'll save time and be able to retrieve the files you want when you want them.

For ideas on how to organize your files, check out the guidance from professional researcher Drew Smith, author of *Organize Your Genealogy: Strategies and Solutions for Every Researcher* (Family Tree Books). Also listen to his tips in the free *Family Tree Magazine* Podcast interview at <familytreemagazine.com/article/episode98>. Get advice for putting pictures in order from *How to Archive Family Photos* (Family Tree Books) by Denise May Levenick.

4 Subscribe to genealogy newsletters and blogs.

How do you stay up-to-date on new genealogy websites and other happenings in the genealogy world (other than reading *Family Tree Magazine*)? Subscribe to RSS feeds or emailed newsletters from the genealogy sites you use most frequently, as well as to research experts and industry insiders. A few of our favorites are GeneaBloggers.com <www.geneabloggers.com>, Genealogy Gems <www.lisalouisecooke.com>, Eastman's Online Genealogy Newsletter <eogn.com> and, of course, the *Family Tree Magazine* newsletter <www.familytreemagazine.com>. Simply go to the website and look for options to sign up or join the feed.

5 Interview elderly relatives.

Genealogists often wait too long to interview older generations. Before you know it, they've taken ill or passed away, or their memories begin to fade. Make it a priority to interview relatives—perhaps starting with the most senior individuals or those in declining health. Make a list of the relatives you most want to ask about family history, in the order you want to contact them, with their contact information. Start reaching out to each in turn to conduct your interviews via email, postal mail, phone or in person. Before each conversation, prepare a list of questions you want to ask.

Record in-person interviews with your smart-phone's audio or video recorder, or use a standalone app. You also can use the free companion apps for genealogy websites MyHeritage <www.myheritage.com> or FamilySearch to record and save interviews directly to individual profiles on your online trees. Just remember to go back in and download a copy of each interview for your files at home.

> The more research you do, the more you realize it's easy to lose track of where you learned what. Having a standard file-naming system makes scanning photos faster and finding them later easier.

6 Digitize old photos—one batch at a time.

Before my parents retired and moved to a smaller home in Florida, my mom set out on a yearlong project to digitize all the family photos, both her own and those inherited from my grandma. It was a massive, time-consuming undertaking. Instead of facing something like that, start now and break the project into smaller chunks: by topic, family, time period or event.

First, choose a scanner that's best for your situation. If you want the flexibility to scan photos wherever you go (even if it's just while sitting on the sofa watching TV), consider a portable option. If you need something that scans in higher resolution or one that saves images in different file formats (like the archival TIF format), look into dedicated flatbed scanners. See the More Online box for links that will help you choose the right scanner for your project. Unexpected opportunities may arise to scan photos on the go, so consider downloading a free photo-scanning app such as Pic Scanner (for iOS) or Shoe-box from Ancestry.com (for Android or iOS). The image quality won't be as good as using a real scanner, but it's better than not capturing the image at all.

Remember to use the same file-naming and digital filing structure for your old photos as for your new ones. Having a standard system makes it faster to scan them and easier to find them later.

7 Subscribe to your dream genealogy website.

What genealogy website subscription is next on your wish list? Ancestry.com or MyHeritage <myheritage.com>? Fold3 <www.fold3.com> for military research or GenealogyBank <www.genealogybank.com> for old newspapers? This year, subscribe to one new website and focus your research efforts there to make your investment worthwhile. Need help deciding? See our Best Websites for Genealogy at <familytreemagazine.com/best-genealogy-websites> and click on the category for the best big websites or another topic of interest.

Next year, continue the subscription if you're still getting a lot out of it. Or cancel it (follow any cancellation instructions to avoid auto-renewal) and choose the next dream website on your list.

8 Heighten your online privacy awareness.

Online privacy is an increasing concern for many people. Read the privacy practices of genealogy websites *before* you use them. For example, the FamilySearch content submission agreement <www.familysearch.org/legal/familysearch-content-submission-agreement> essentially gives FamilySearch license to use your uploaded documents and images in any way it chooses. Other genealogy websites have similar terms in their fine print. For example, find privacy policies for Ancestry.com at <ancestry.com/cs/legal/privacystatement> and Findmypast.com at <www.findmypast.com/content/privacy-policy>.

In addition to knowing how a company or website uses information you contribute, it's important to know what information the site shows publicly (such as username and/or contact information). Look in the site's account or privacy settings to see what you can change or opt out of sharing publicly. For example, on FamilySearch under your username, click the Settings link to see your name, username, display name and birth date, along with a box you can check to make this information public or keep it private.

Lastly, familiarize yourself with what personal information gets shared on various genealogy sites. Most family tree websites don't typically post information publicly on living people in your tree, but don't assume this is the policy. Check it out, and if you're unsure, err on the side of caution so you don't accidentally reveal personal info about living relatives (including their names) without their permission.

9 Pay attention to your DNA match messages.

Many in the genealogy community complain that people who take DNA tests seem to ignore their messages from matches. If that's you, log into your account to see if you have any messages. Update your contact information as needed, especially your email address if it has changed. As new people get tested and their data is added to the DNA database, it's possible you could have new matches waiting—you just have to pay attention and stay connected.

10 Create and maintain a master family tree.

Having one master family tree will keep your research organized and make it easier to check and share your information. It also can help you see where you're missing key data (or the sources that support it). Consider keeping your master tree in software on your computer, which secures your information, as well as posting copies of your tree online.

Genealogy software options include RootsMagic <www.rootsmagic.com>, which offers free and premium options and has full sync-ability with Ancestry.com trees. Legacy Family Tree <www.legacyfamilytree.com> also offers a free version of its software. Family Tree Maker software <www.mackiev.com/ftm>, which syncs with Ancestry.com, is available from Software MacKiev. MyHeritage has free desktop tree software, Family Tree Builder <www.myheritage.com/family-tree-builder>, that syncs with your online tree at MyHeritage. Most programs now offer mobile apps you can use to check or edit your family tree on the go.

You can plant your family tree online for free on many genealogy websites. At FamilySearch, WikiTree <www.wikitree.com> and WeRelate <www.werelate.org>, you're contributing to a master "community tree," with one record per shared ancestor. That means others may make changes to what you post and you may not be able to download your research as a tree file.

On sites such as Ancestry.com, Findmypast and MyHeritage, you can build an "independent" tree for free; other people can make changes only if you invite them to do so. These sites will give you hints to records and other trees that match your ancestors, but you'll need to subscribe to gain full access to features such as reviewing historical records or, for MyHeritage, to exceed 250 people on your tree.

11

Set up a genealogy-only email address.

You probably already maintain separate e-mail accounts for work and personal communication, but it's helpful to have a dedicated address for genealogy, too. That keeps those genealogy website notifications, your correspondence with potential cousins, and responses to your record requests from getting lost. Set up a free email account with Gmail <www.gmail.com> or Yahoo! Mail <www.yahoo.com>.

If you do use your work email for genealogy, stop. Your employer can review your email, and if you leave your job, you won't be able to keep saved communications.

Whatever email accounts you set up, protect against hacking with strong, unique passwords. Remembering all those strong passwords (with random capital letters, characters and strings of numbers) isn't easy, though. Consider using a password manager such as LastPass <www.lastpass.com>, Dashlane <www.dashlane.com> and RoboForm <www.roboform.com>.

MORE ONLINE

@ **Web Content**
- Get your research organized <familytreemagazine.com/article/win-the-paper-chase>
- Organize your genealogy email <familytreemagazine.com/article/organize-your-genealogy-email>
- Choosing the right scanner for you <familytreemagazine.com/article/the-skinny-on-scanners>
- Cutting paper clutter <familytreemagazine.com/organization/end-the-genealogy-paper-trail>
- Backing up your genealogy <familytreemagazine.com/article/genealogy-backup-basics>
- Oral history recording apps <familytreemagazine.com/article/quick-guide-oral-history-recording-apps>

12

Search offline.

It's easy to get into the habit of limiting your researching to historical records that are online. But many important records *aren't* online. Make a list of the records you want to find and order. Set goals for how many to check off your list each month (or year)—and a budget for ordering copies.

As you tackle each item, consult any online indexes to those records to determine where the originals are and how to order them. If those records aren't even indexed online, use FamilySearch's wiki <www.familysearch.org/wiki>, the FamilySearch catalog <www.familysearch.org/search/catalog> and your favorite web browser to locate and request copies of offline vital records, probate records, deeds, newspapers and more.

13

Seek help.

Navigating genealogy records can be tricky. Record-keeping, record maintenance and privacy laws may limit what you can find for some record types, regions and time periods. Seek out expert knowledge to save time, advance your research and learn the idiosyncrasies of various records and repositories. Attend genealogy conferences and seminars; take an online class or attend a virtual conference with Family Tree University <familytreeuniversity.com> or attend the meetings of a local genealogical or historical society.

TIP: Use a cloud service to automate backing up your computer files whenever your computer is online.

16 Record your own story.

Genealogists focus so much on the past, but sometimes forget to record history as it's made in the present. Start writing down your own life story, a little at a time, in regular intervals. Record memories from your childhood and major life milestones. Then, starting this year and in each succeeding year, document the year's highlights: births of children or grandchildren, travel, accomplishments and more. Use a book such as *Story of My Life: A Workbook for Preserving Your Legacy* by Sunny Jane Morton (Family Tree Books) to prompt memories and keep them all in one place. The book is available both as a full-sized, softbound workbook and a writeable PDF. If you're not a writer, use a voice-recording app to record your life stories.

14 Organize your family heirlooms.

Photos, jewelry, furniture, wedding gowns, scrapbooks and newspaper clippings are a few of the items you might inherit from relatives. Start keeping better track of them. Write down information about the history behind each item as you receive it. (Our Artifacts and Heirlooms, and Heirloom Inventory forms can help; find them at **<familytreemagazine.com/info/oralhistory forms>**.) Store items properly so they don't deteriorate over time. Attach images of these items—and anything you learn about the family from them—to personal profiles in your family tree software. For more advice, see Denise May Levenick's *How to Archive Family Keepsakes* (Family Tree Books).

15 Back up your records regularly.

You never know when your computer hard drive is going to crash or succumb to disaster or theft. Back up your digital genealogy files and photos at least once a month—and immediately after you make a lot of additions or changes to your files. Save copies to an external hard drive and to a second medium that's in a physically different location from your original files and primary backup.

A good option for that second medium is to activate an automated cloud backup service such as Apple iCloud **<www.apple.com/icloud>**, Backblaze **<www.backblaze.com>**, Carbonite **<www.carbonite.com>** or SugarSync **<www.sugarsync.com>**. Mac users can go with Time Machine **<support.apple.com/en-us/HT201250>** or Mac Carbon Copy Cloner **<www.bombich.com>**.

17 Plan a family get-together.

One of the best parts of researching your family history is sharing it with relatives. If your family doesn't currently get together regularly, consider planning a one-time or annual reunion—or offer to share your family history if someone *else* will plan the event. Consider creative ways for imparting what you know: through photo displays, PowerPoint slide shows, games with ancestral trivia or photos, and foods from your family's heritage. Check out tips for planning a successful reunion at **<familytreemagazine.com/article/10-steps-to-family-reunion-success>**. ∎

Wisconsin-based freelance writer and editor **DANA MCCULLOUGH** is the author of *Unofficial Guide to Family-Search.org* (Family Tree Books). Visit her website at **<www.danamccullough.com>**.

All in a Day's Work

If all you've got is a Saturday to organize your genealogy, make it count with these tips for a successful one-day organization project.

by ANDREW KOCH

Keeping your research organized is a bit like saving for retirement: The best time to start was yesterday, but the second-best time is today. It's much easier to organize your research as you go.

But since many of us have been accumulating data and documents for years (even decades) and have other obligations, it can be easy to fall behind.

Let's say this upfront: You probably can't organize *all* your research in a single day. Sustainable organization requires a thoughtful plan and constant maintenance, plus a not-insignificant amount of time. But if one day is all you can spare to get your research organized, here's how to make the most of it.

BEFORE THE DAY

To have the most efficient work day possible, you'll need to prepare days or even weeks in advance. Here are some ways to set yourself up for a productive day ahead of time.

CLEAR THE DAY

If you can help it, make this day *only* about your genealogy. Having other tasks or events (appointments, errands, parties or social engagements, chores, etc.) during this time will disrupt your flow, so avoid them as best you can. Obtain any necessary child- or petcare, and submit any time-off requests to your employer. Maybe even set up an email away message or note on your front door, or inform relatives and friends that you'll be out-of-touch and nose-down in genealogy work.

CREATE GOALS

With such a narrow time window, you'll need to decide what you want to accomplish. What specifically can you do in that day to feel successful? What do you *really* hope to achieve?

Not being upfront with their goals is one of the most common mistakes people make when tackling an organization project, according to professional organizer Lahni Carney. "We see this in clients who make the process a lot longer than it needs to be with an inability to make decisions, wanting to change things over and over," says Carney, who owns organization-consulting service Clutterless Home Solutions <www.clutterlesshomesolutions.com>. "It's very important that clients and everyone involved are on board, or else the project won't be as successful."

Write down your goals for the day, and be as specific as possible. We've written before about creating "S.M.A.R.T" goals, which are:
- **Specific** (i.e., narrow in scope)
- **Measurable** (have clear criteria for whether or not they are completed)
- **Achievable/Attainable** or **Actionable** (can be implemented by you)
- **Realistic** (can reasonably be done with the available time and resources) or **Relevant** (fit into your larger goals)
- **Time-bound** (have a deadline)

The sidebar on page 17 lists some goal ideas that could reasonably be accomplished in a single day. Though not all of them meet the S.M.A.R.T. criteria, you can tailor them to do so and reflect your own research.

Remember, too, that the focus for this day is *organization*, not finding documents. Your goals should be focused on organizing the materials you already have, not searching for new ones or filling in any holes in your family story. "Start small. Choose one aspect of your genealogy you want to organize better," says Gena Philibert-Ortega <www.genagenealogy.com>, professional genealogy researcher and instructor of Family Tree University's "Organize Your Genealogy Research" course. "Just focus on that and not all your genealogy research."

> Looking for a longer-term research plan? See our guides to researching an ancestor in a week and to planning a whole month of genealogy <www.family treemagazine.com/research/7-day-genealogy-research-plan> and <www. familytreemagazine.com/research/genealogy-research-skills>.

JULIE BARNETT

To have the most efficient work day possible, you'll need to prepare days or even weeks in advance.

PRIORITIZE YOUR TIME

Certain research tasks are more important than others, and (with limited time) you'll have to place higher value on some over others. To help triage, create a "must-do" list of your most pertinent, highest-priority tasks for the day, as well as a "would be nice" list. That way, you'll focus on the most important items first, while also creating a list of tasks to pursue if you finish that high-priority list but still have time left.

One framework for prioritizing tasks is the Eisenhower Matrix <www.todoist.com/productivity-methods/eisenhower-matrix>. Named after the general-turned-president Dwight Eisenhower, this method evaluates to-do items using two major criteria: urgency (i.e., timeliness) and importance. It then creates a four-quadrant matrix that dictates what to do with tasks that fit into either category:

	Urgent	**Not Urgent**
Important	Do this first	Schedule to do later
Not Important	Delegate*	Don't do

*The lone researcher probably doesn't have a staff of employees to delegate to! But you might find a tool that can automate tasks that are urgent but not important.

You won't need military efficiency to have a successful organization day. But thinking of your tasks through this lens might help you determine what's really worth your limited time.

Also schedule your day to take best advantage of your most-productive times. Even though I'm a night owl, I like to front-load work days with tasks so I can gather momentum and capitalize on being fresh.

GATHER MATERIALS

You want to maximize your organization day. Trips to the store or time spent rummaging through your house for supplies can be a huge time suck. So once you have a goal, collect any physical items you'll need: file folders and tabs, a scanner, form printouts, a filing cabinet, boxes/papers/photos/documents/media cards you want to sort, refreshments, items to make the day more fun or comfortable, and so on. Don't forget to charge the electronic items you'll need throughout the day, and obtain any needed replacement batteries.

DURING THE DAY

It's finally here—your big organizing day. Here's how to make it productive and efficient.

TAKE SHORT BREAKS

You're not a machine. To do your best work, you need to periodically rest to keep your brain and body sharp.

What does that look like? When looking at a whole day, I often schedule breaks like I did when I worked an hourly-wage retail job. Per company policy, I had to take one 15-minute break every four hours and one 30-minute break every six hours. This model was likely designed to comply with labor laws, but it does create a nice balance of focused work and rest.

Another popular scheduling method is the Pomodoro technique, designed by Francesco Cirillo in the 1980s <www.francescocirillo.com>. In it, you spend 25 minutes straight on a specific task, then break for five minutes. Every four cycles (essentially, every two hours), you take a longer break—say, 15 or 30 minutes. This allows you to enter a space of "deep work" for a concentrated amount of time, then giving you dedicated time to lose focus.

See the sidebar for sample day schedules using each technique. In the chart, the one I use is called the "15/4 Method."

14 Organization Projects You Can DO IN A DAY

- ✓ Standardize file names (either digital or physical)

- ✓ Standardize place names, dates, or personal names in your online tree/software program

- ✓ Color-code folders (either digital or physical)

- ✓ Fill out new, "clean" research forms to outline the scope of your research and what progress you've made

- ✓ Scan several piles of photos or documents

- ✓ Sort through a specific box(es) of unorganized materials

- ✓ Create an inventory of records you have for each direct-line ancestor, and what you still need

- ✓ Download record images of a certain type (e.g., federal censuses) for all known direct-line ancestors; name and sort them as you go

- ✓ Audit your existing filing system: How are your files currently organized? What is the scope of your "unorganized" pile?

- ✓ Gather all your physical research—research notes, copies of records, boxes of unsorted materials, photos—in one place

- ✓ Collect digital files from multiple drives/servers onto one device

- ✓ Create a specific genealogy report: Retrieve and curate facts. (Leave any additional research items for another time.)

- ✓ Create and implement a digital backup system: Investigate options and make any needed purchases. Create a schedule for regular backups

- ✓ Move data between trees or software: Ensure materials copied over correctly, and re-attach media and sources as necessary

5 PROJECTS to AVOID

The following goals will set you up for failure:

- ✗ **Scanning *all* photos or documents:** This may be physically impossible in your allotted time, depending on the speed of your scanner and how many things need scanned. Instead, outline a specific set of files or papers to work on that day. Alternatively, make your goal auditing your photo/document collection and creating a scanning plan that you'll work through later.

- ✗ **Creating *and* implementing a new filing system:** Designing an organization system in a day is one thing, but sorting all your files into it in those same eight hours is another. You'll likely only have time to do one or the other.

- ✗ **Adding metadata to *all* digital files:** This could be hundreds or even thousands of files. A more-reasonable goal would be reviewing your digital files and developing templates for file names and metadata.

- ✗ **Adding source citations to *all* materials:** As before, you could simply review the current status of your research and make list of what documentation is still needed.

- ✗ **Doing actual records research:** This is far too open-ended. You could easily get pulled in different directions, using up your limited time. As with other distractions, make a list of to-do items that surface as you're organizing.

YOUR ORGANIZATION DAY:
Two Sample Schedules

To do your best work, you'll need to take breaks. This article describes two different models for how to do so. Here's what each might look like in practice during an 8-to-5 session.

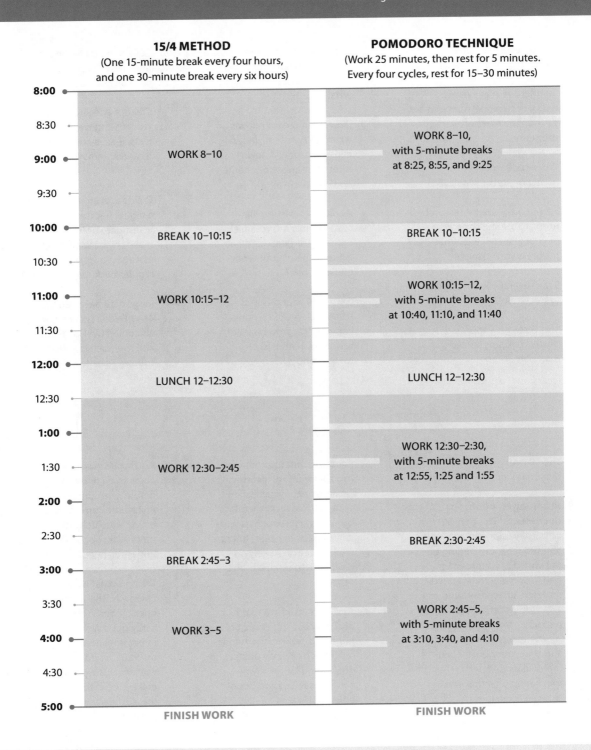

15/4 METHOD
(One 15-minute break every four hours,
and one 30-minute break every six hours)

8:00

8:30

9:00 — WORK 8–10

9:30

10:00 — BREAK 10–10:15

10:30

11:00 — WORK 10:15–12

11:30

12:00 — LUNCH 12–12:30

12:30

1:00

1:30 — WORK 12:30–2:45

2:00

2:30

— BREAK 2:45–3

3:00

3:30

4:00 — WORK 3–5

4:30

5:00 — FINISH WORK

POMODORO TECHNIQUE
(Work 25 minutes, then rest for 5 minutes.
Every four cycles, rest for 15–30 minutes)

WORK 8–10,
with 5-minute breaks
at 8:25, 8:55, and 9:25

BREAK 10–10:15

WORK 10:15–12,
with 5-minute breaks
at 10:40, 11:10, and 11:40

LUNCH 12–12:30

WORK 12:30–2:30,
with 5-minute breaks
at 12:55, 1:25 and 1:55

BREAK 2:30-2:45

WORK 2:45–5,
with 5-minute breaks
at 3:10, 3:40, and 4:10

FINISH WORK

Find all *Family Tree*'s tips for organizing your research at <www.familytreemagazine.com/organize-genealogy>.

MAKE IT FEEL SPECIAL

Treat yourself to a fun breakfast or lunch, or make dinner plans for after. Or maybe drink your favorite coffee or tea (or something stronger later in the day!). While you work, you could listen to your favorite or long-anticipated music, TV show, podcast, or audiobook.

TAKE CARE OF YOUR BODY

Sleep well the night before, and stay well-fed and -hydrated. Wear comfortable clothes and shoes. Use a kneeling pad if you'll be on your knees or on the floor, and grab a comfortable chair if you'll be sitting.

AVOID DISTRACTIONS

Stick to your goals (attempting just one at a time), and stay far away from those oh-so-easy "rabbit holes." Only review the materials you're organizing well enough to know what they are.

"Focus is incredibly important," Carney says. "The best advice I give to clients is to finish the project they're working on before you move onto another. If you start with too much, you'll get overwhelmed and end up with a bigger project than you started with."

As stated earlier, *do not try to do any actual research on this day*. As research tasks arise, make a list of to-do items for another time. For example, while organizing my family's home files, I made a list of files that I needed to obtain physical copies of—I didn't interrupt my organizing project to print them out.

CREATE A SYSTEM THAT WORKS FOR *YOU*

If part of your project is creating an organization system for your research, think about how you'll use that system moving forward. Make decisions based on the tools and goals you're already familiar with.

That system will look different for everyone; one size won't fit all. "Don't try to take on something that isn't intuitive for you and that you aren't comfortable with," says Philibert-Ortega. "You are successful at organizing when you choose systems that you will return to time and time again and not what someone tells you, you should use."

AFTER THE DAY

Even when your organization day is done, you can take some steps to stay organized and keep moving your research forward.

DOCUMENT YOUR JOURNEY

Take before and after pictures to share with family or on social media. This will help you feel accomplished and hold yourself accountable—and maybe even inspire others to take on a similar project.

ACCEPT ANY LIMITATIONS

Don't beat yourself if you didn't accomplish everything you wanted. Work will never fully be done; even the most organized, "put-together" genealogist has unorganized parts of their research.

Some progress is better than none. You're just competing against yourself—your ultimate goal is that your research is more organized today than it was yesterday. And you can always schedule another organization day if necessary!

FOLLOW UP ON ANY ACTION ITEMS

If you've followed the advice thus far, you will have made a list of any to-do items that came up during your organization project. These will often be smaller to-do's, but could also be open-ended (like researching a particular family line more).

For Philibert-Ortega, even small increments of time can help. "At the beginning or the end of my work day, I take at least 15 to 30 minutes and organize, whether that's organizing digital files, or going through my paper folders and photographs," she says. "We live in an era where we have so many demands on our time, but most of us can dedicate 15 minutes to focused organization."

MAINTAIN

Don't backslide! Continue to use and develop your organization system. "The most important way to stay organized is to put things away immediately, and not just set it down to do later," Carney says. "This is the no.1 reason people are disorganized. Build up the habit to put things away *right away* in the 'home' you've established." ●

Andrew Koch is the editor of *Family Tree Magazine*. His work desk isn't as organized as he'd like, but he's setting aside an upcoming Saturday to work on it.

GO for the GOAL

Stay on task with a genealogy resolution for each month. We've got your game plan with simple, customizable steps.

by SUNNY JANE MORTON

f you're like me, as each new year settles in, you fill the blank pages of your calendar quickly—too quickly. But this year, elevate your family history research to a priority worthy of its own spot in your schedule. Whether you mark off 15 minutes a day, an hour a week, or a weekend binge every month is up to you.

Not sure what to do in that time? Too busy to think about next month, let alone six months from now? We hear you, and we're here to help. Here's your guide to planning an orderly, comprehensive and time-flexible series of essential family history tasks for the coming year. And we've broken each goal into several achievable steps. Choose one task each month if your time is short, or go all-out and try several. Re-order the monthly assignments as needed to fit your schedule, lifestyle and budget. The important thing is to keep your genealogy calendar time slot full of family history tasks you love (or need) to do.

JANUARY Get organized

Start the year off right by organizing what you've already learned about your family. Take these steps:

- **Set up computer file folders.** Create a genealogy file on your computer (if you don't already have one). Add subfiles for each surname you're researching. As you add new surnames, you could add folders at the same organizational level (Plan A) or nest them within major surnames of interest (Plan B). Plan A is simpler; Plan B mimics your family structure.

Within each surname folder, add subfolders for nuclear family groups as needed. This will be especially helpful if you're studying multiple generations of a family. (If you've already got an electronic family history filing system, tidy it up.)

- **Populate subfolders with files.** Add digitized photos and documents, research reports and other materials relating to each person or family group. Download copies of records attached to ancestors in your online trees, which ensures you'll have copies of the files even if your subscription expires or the site goes down.

- **Download raw DNA data.** Do this for all tests you manage. Stash your raw data in a DNA subfolder in your main genealogy file.

- **Start (or update) your family tree** online or in genealogy software. Be sure all your discoveries get added to the appropriate individuals. If your tree "lives" in software on your computer, activate any syncing features so linked online trees stay current.

- **Back up your computer and external drives.** This protects you against computer failure or other loss. You could do regular, manual backups to multiple locations (cloud-based storage such as Dropbox <www.dropbox.com> and hardware-based using an external hard drive). Automate this process—and make it continuous—by using a cloud-based backup system such as Backblaze <www.backblaze.com>, Carbonite <www.carbonite.com> or iDrive <www.idrive.com>.

- **Take your level of organization up a notch** with Drew Smith's *Organize Your Genealogy* guidebook (Family Tree Books) <familytreemagazine.com/store/organize-your-genealogy-paperback>.

FEBRUARY Reconstruct a family

Cold-weather weekends are great for research binge sessions. This month, you'll use records to reconstruct a family. This is a perfect next step after organizing what you already know, and can rapidly expand your genealogy knowledge.

- **Identify a family or branch on your tree** for which you have little information.

- **Put a working family tree on genealogy websites** you subscribe to. This activates automated record hinting, which means you'll get hints and links to censuses and vital records that may match your ancestors.

- **Carefully review record hints** for each nuclear family, beginning with the most recent generations. Watching for records that match on multiple, specific

parameters, such as a spouse's name and the names and approximate ages of children. Attach records to their tree profiles only when you have a high degree of confidence in the match—but keep track of "maybes" for later reference.

- **Go to each family member's tree profile** after exhausting record hints. Look for record gaps such as missing census years or dates of birth, marriage or death. Run targeted searches for records likely to fill these gaps. Identify as many records about the same vital event as possible (for example, an obituary, death certificate and tombstone inscription). Multiple, independent sources for these vital events strengthen your tree.

- **Clean up loose ends as you go.** For example, if you find a second

marriage, determine how the first one ended. Try to identify which children belonged to each partner and ensure the relationships are correct on your tree (record hinting systems may automatically attach children to step-parents when they appear together in records).

- **Identify other sources.** As needed, visit different genealogy websites or research specific record types to learn about records covering your ancestor's time and place, and how you can get them.

MARCH Find female ancestors

Observe Women's History Month by paying extra attention to your female forbears. In the past, women appeared in records with far less frequency than men, and even less often under their own names (a woman might be "Mrs. Charles Smith" instead of Fannie Jones). That's why you may have so many "dangling women" on your tree, for whom you have only a birth year.

- **Focus on one or two female ancestors.** Dig into the records of husbands, siblings (especially brothers), parents and children. Look for maiden surnames in relatives' obituaries. See whether marriage records (especially for a first marriage) and children's birth records mention her maiden name. In older records, look for marriage bonds or a woman's appearance as a widow in her husband's military pension files.

- **Take a mitochondrial DNA test,** available from Family Tree DNA <www.familytreedna.com> to more deeply explore your maternal lineage. If you test early enough in March, you'll likely have your results by Mother's Day (the test takes about six to eight weeks to process).

Both men and women carry their mothers' mtDNA, but only women pass mtDNA on to their children. An mtDNA test traces your maternal line's deep ethnic origins. You'll get an idea where in the world your direct maternal line (mother's mother's mother) is on this maternal line. You also may benefit by reviewing mtDNA matches. Just keep in mind that the testing pool is small and mtDNA rarely mutates, so you won't be able to tell how closely related you are to your matches.

> April 25 is National DNA Day—take advantage of special sales to order DNA tests for yourself and your relatives.

APRIL Do more with DNA

April 25 is National DNA Day—a great time to order DNA tests on sale—for yourself and for relatives. Start with autosomal DNA testing, offered by AncestryDNA <ancestry.com/dna>, MyHeritageDNA <www.myheritage.com/dna> and 23andMe <www.23andme.com>. This can identify matches on both sides of the tester's family who have a common ancestor four to six generations in the past. YDNA tests, which follow your direct paternal line (father's father's father, etc.), are useful for finding cousins with shared ancestors along your paternal line.

- **Ask relatives to test**. Their DNA may help you solve family history mysteries. A person who's not interested in testing for genealogy research may still be dying to learn his ethnicity breakdown. Respectfully address any privacy concerns and maintain confidentiality when relatives test. Though you may have access to their results, it's their DNA to share (or not) as they wish.

- **Message matches.** If you've already tested, work to learn your relationship with your closest DNA matches by contacting them through the testing site to compare family trees. Search for common names and places of birth. Also examine your shared matches. Log what you learn in a spreadsheet or in the notes field for each match.

- **Use new tools.** Upload your raw DNA data to collaborative genetic genealogy websites such as GEDmatch <www.gedmatch.com> to find additional matches and use analysis tools. Also consider uploading your DNA data to testing company websites that accept uploads (currently, they're MyHeritage DNA, Living DNA and Family Tree DNA).

- **Explore health insights.** Take 23andMe's Health + Ancestry test or upload your raw DNA data to an inexpensive service such as Promethease <www.promethease.com> or Livewello <www.livewello.com>. Share the results with your doctor—remember that these tests don't have diagnostic power.

- **Join a DNA study** focused on a surname, haplogroup, ethnicity or geographic origin. Check Family Tree DNA <www.familytreedna.com/projects.aspx> and Cyndi's List <cyndislist.com/surnames/dna>.

When doing DNA research, be prepared for unanticipated discoveries. Communicate tactfully with matches, especially concerning previously unknown relationships. If you think you've discovered information that may affect living relatives, you might consult a professional genetic genealogist to confirm your results. Then consider carefully whether and how to share what you've learned.

MAY Do a house history

This month, take time to learn the history of your own home or another building significant to your family history. You may be able to learn the original layout of a property, when it was built or remodeled, how much your family paid, and who else has lived there. If you're so inclined, compile a binder with your own house history and leave a copy as a gift for the next owner—this might even influence potential buyers looking for a special new home.

• **Start online.** The county clerk's or recorder's website might have an online real-estate database you can search by address for clues to when the structure was built, its lot number and sales history.

• **Trace property transfers** through deeds. If you can go to the local courthouse or a library with microfilmed deeds (or if you're lucky enough to find county records digitized at FamilySearch), research ownership history by finding the most recent deed and using it to identify the previous owner and deed. Then look at that deed and then the previous one, and so forth. This is called following a chain of title, and it may take you back to the original owner. Those documents may hold a property description and other interesting tidbits.

• **Look for old maps.** You also might find plat maps or other maps from the time your ancestors lived there on sites such as the David Rumsey Historical Map Collection <www.davidrumsey.com>. Fire insurance map collections such as Sanborn Maps, many of which are available on the Library of Congress website <loc.gov/collections/sanborn-maps> may reveal details such as construction materials, uses (such as "store" or "bakery") and what the neighborhood looked like at the time.

• **Document residents** in records. Research who lived in the house in city directories and censuses. You can search for the address as a keyword in digitized city directories on sites such as Ancestry and MyHeritage. Then search for the residents' names in US census records.

• **Check out news that happened nearby.** Search for the property's address and residents' names in digitized newspapers on sites such as Newspapers.com <www.newspapers.com> and GenealogyBank <www.genealogybank.com>.

tip Find links to city directories (some, free) at the Online Historical Directories Website <sites.google.com/site/onlinedirectorysite>.

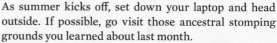

JUNE Go outside

As summer kicks off, set down your laptop and head outside. If possible, go visit those ancestral stomping grounds you learned about last month.

• **Stroll through old family neighborhoods.** Go looking for landmarks that may have been around during your relatives' day: homes, churches, monuments and even trees. Try to spot the oldest buildings and imagine the spaces between them before they were filled. If you have family addresses from old records, try to locate the address as it exists today. Is the home still there? How has the neighborhood changed?

• **Visit relatives' graves**. A trip to local cemeteries could turn up relatives. Study graves for genealogical clues: birth and death dates, and extended family burials nearby. Take photos of inscriptions and clustered graves. (Gravestone rubbings are illegal in many place. Unless you have express permission from cemetery staff, just take pictures.) If graves look like someone's actively caring for them you may have a heritage-minded cousin living nearby.

• **Stop at the library.** Your family's hometown library could be a unique resource for neighborhood maps, old school yearbooks and local histories.

• **Let Google Earth <google.com/earth> show you around if you can't leave town.** Enter an address or approximate location. Where available, use Street View to surround yourself with a 360-degree view of the neighborhood. Cemetery websites such as Find A Grave <www.findagrave.com> or BillionGraves <billiongraves.com> can help you locate and even virtually tour your relatives' final resting places.

JULY Reconnect with relatives

Summertime often means family reunions; a chance to catch up with distant cousins. You also might have a bit more leisure time to plan get-togethers.

- **Take the lead.** If you're hosting a reunion, bless you. If you're attending, offer to help with something, such as managing door prizes, handling the event invite on Facebook, bringing desserts or creating a heritage display.

- **Schedule time with relatives.** There's no need for grand plans. Have dinner with a favorite aunt, go on a walk with your cousin, invite the kids for a pool party or plan a siblings' getaway weekend.

- **Ask about family history.** Oral history interviews strengthen relationships and benefit your family history research with firsthand knowledge. You could sit down with Great-aunt Marie at a reunion or schedule a separate time. Let her know ahead of time what you'd like to talk about: her own life stories, memories of older relatives or her cache of family artifacts. Ask if you can scan her old family photos, and if you can record the conversation (smartphone apps make it easy).

- **Use technology.** If you can't meet in person (or you want to keep in touch after the reunion), bridge the distance via Skype, telephone, a personal email or an old-fashioned letter. Share a favorite memory of the person and say what you appreciate about him. You also could send a copy of a favorite family photo or invite the person to view your online family tree.

AUGUST Travel into history

Incorporate your love of heritage into summer road trips before the season fades away. The genealogist's ultimate destination is often a research library, such as the Family History Library in Salt Lake City <www.familysearch.org/locations/saltlakecity-library> or the Genealogy Center at the Allen County Public Library in Fort Wayne, Ind <www.genealogycenter.org>. Also investigate state archives and local libraries where your ancestors lived.

- **Prepare for a library trip.** Before you start your library research, identify questions you hope to answer and which library resources can help. Find out about hours, parking, copying materials and other logistics. If you want to use any rare or manuscript items, call to confirm they'll be available for your use.

- **Tour a living history destination.** This is a great activity, particularly if you'll have traveling companions. History destinations immerse visitors in the sights, sounds, smells and tastes of the past. You might be able to watch costumed artisans bake bread on a hearth or hammer on a blacksmith's anvil. Or, perhaps you can ride in a horse-drawn carriage, canal boat, Model T car or narrow gauge rail car. Find a museum related to your family's history at <www.alhfam.org/museum-links>.

- **Looking for a simpler way to travel into the past?** Curl up in a hammock or on the beach with a good historical novel. Well-researched and written books can transport you to another time and place.

tip

Socializing with other genealogists at a class or conference is a great way to reinvigorate your love of family history research.

2 YEARLY GOALS AT A GLANCE

JANUARY Get organized.
- ☐ Set up your computer file folders.
- ☐ Populate subfolders with files.
- ☐ Download raw DNA data for all tests you manage.
- ☐ Start a family tree online or in genealogy software.
- ☐ Back up your computer and external drives.
- ☐ Follow tips from a guidebook like *Organize Your Genealogy*.

FEBRUARY Reconstruct a family.
- ☐ Choose a family to focus on.
- ☐ Put a working family tree on genealogy websites to which you subscribe.
- ☐ Carefully review record hints for each nuclear family.
- ☐ Go to each family member's tree profile and search for records.
- ☐ Look for errors and fix loose ends.
- ☐ Identify other sources covering your ancestor's time and place.

MARCH Find female ancestors.
- ☐ Focus on a female ancestor or two. Dig into the records of husbands, siblings, parents and children.
- ☐ Take a mitochondrial DNA test to explore your maternal line.

APRIL Do more with DNA.
- ☐ Ask relatives to test.
- ☐ Message your DNA matches.
- ☐ Transfer your raw DNA to collaborative genetic genealogy websites.
- ☐ Explore health-related insights such as your genetic health risks, carrier status and more.
- ☐ Join a DNA study focused on a surname, haplogroup, ethnicity or geographic origins.

MAY Do a house history.
- ☐ Start online with the county clerk or recorder's website.
- ☐ Trace property transfers through deeds.
- ☐ Look for old maps.
- ☐ Document residents in records.
- ☐ Check out old newspapers for local history.

JUNE Go outside.
- ☐ Stroll through old family neighborhoods looking for landmarks from your relatives' day.
- ☐ Visit relatives' graves.
- ☐ Stop at the library in your family's hometown.
- ☐ Virtually visit ancestral towns with Google Earth <google.com/earth>.

JULY Reconnect with relatives.
- ☐ Host or help with a family reunion.
- ☐ Schedule time to spend with relatives.
- ☐ Ask a relative about family history.
- ☐ Use technology to keep in touch.

AUGUST Travel into history.
- ☐ Prepare for a library trip by identifying your questions and available resources.
- ☐ Tour a living history destination.
- ☐ Read a historical novel that's related to your family heritage.

SEPTEMBER Improve your skills.
- ☐ Go to a meeting of a local genealogical or historical society.
- ☐ Take an online class in a new genealogy skill.
- ☐ Listen to a genealogy podcast.

OCTOBER Give back.
- ☐ Contribute tombstone photos and inscriptions to crowdsourced collections.
- ☐ Respond to others' requests for tombstone images.
- ☐ Index or transcribe genealogical records.

NOVEMBER Tell your stories.
- ☐ Choose an ancestor you're excited to write about and review your research about that person.
- ☐ Gain a sense of your ancestor's story by creating a timeline or drafting a narrative.
- ☐ Rewrite, edit and proofread your work so it's ready to share.
- ☐ Work on an album, a family tree for display, or other another family story project.

DECEMBER Celebrate traditions.
- ☐ Enrich seasonal celebrations with favorite family traditions.
- ☐ Create a display that honors relatives who've passed.

ADD YOUR OWN GOALS HERE:

- ☐ _____
- ☐ _____
- ☐ _____
- ☐ _____
- ☐ _____

SEPTEMBER Improve your skills

Take yourself back to school this month. What new genealogical skill would you like to learn or brush up on? Consider these options:

- **Drop into the meeting** of a local genealogical or historical society. Search online for such groups by using the name of your city or county and the phrase genealogical society or historical society, look for notices at the local library, or see <ngsmembers.ngsgenealogy.org/Societies-and-Organizations-Directory2>. You may meet kindred spirits, find out about classes, and discover opportunities to help your community preserve its history. Be prepared to pay a minimal fee to visit or join the group.

- **Take an online class.** Hone a skill you need to move your family history research to the next level with a class. For example: using YDNA test results, searching genealogy websites more effectively, or reading old German records. Check out offerings for topics you have in mind at Family Tree University <familytreemagazine.com/university>.

- **Listen to a podcast.** These online "radio shows" bring you genealogy education in an entertaining, portable format. Naturally, we love the free monthly Family Tree Magazine Podcast <familytreemagazine.com/podcasts>, packed with tips from our editors and contributors. This podcast is hosted by Lisa Louise Cooke, who also hosts the free Genealogy Gems Podcast <lisalouisecooke.com/podcasts>. The Genealogy Guys <genealogyguys.com> offer two educational podcasts. Find these and others via Apple Podcasts, Google Play Music, Spotify or your favorite podcast app. Or listen from your computer by visiting the websites and clicking on a recent episode.

OCTOBER Give back

As you celebrate Family History Month, an unofficial observation by many genealogy organizations, take the opportunity to make family history more accessible.

- **Contribute tombstone photos to crowdsourced collections** at Find A Grave <www.findagrave.com> or BillionGraves <www.billiongraves.com>. To find a nearby cemetery at Find A Grave, look under Cemeteries> Browse; at BillionGraves, go to Research> Cemetery Search. Both sites also have mobile apps. Look for cemeteries with few tombstones already listed, and follow instructions to upload gravestone photos.

- **Respond to others' requests for tombstone images.** You can help someone who can't travel to a burial ground near you. At BillionGraves, an orange icon on the cemetery map means someone has requested a photo. Select that cemetery, scroll down and click on a Photo Request and follow the instructions. At Find A Grave, go to an individual cemetery's home page and click on Photo Requests.

- **Index or transcribe records.** Ask about local indexing projects at the society you visited last month. Join the 1.2 million volunteers who transcribe digitized records via FamilySearch Indexing <www.familysearch.org/indexing>. Or, help indexing and transcription initiatives of the National Archives <archives.gov/citizen-archivist>, Smithsonian <transcription.si.edu>, or the Holocaust Memorial Museum <www.ushmm.org/online/world-memory-project> to name a few of the many organizations looking for volunteers.

Writing your ancestor's life story gives you an opportunity to organize, analyze and put into print the family history discoveries you've made.

NOVEMBER
Tell your stories

It's NaNoWriMo, National Novel Writing Month <nanowrimo.org>. Why not write your ancestors' stories, or even just one ancestor's story? Create projects you can give as holiday gifts next month—you'll thank yourself later (and so will others). And writing your ancestor's life story gives you an opportunity to organize, analyze and put into print the family history discoveries you've made.

- **Choose an ancestor you're excited to write about.** Review your collection of documents about that person, as well as information in your tree, research logs and notes you've kept (this'll be easier if you've kept up with January's organizing system).
- **Gain a sense of your ancestor's story.** Create a timeline or draft a narrative of your ancestor's life, based on the evidence from old records. Analyze conflicts in the evidence and resolve them as best you can by finding additional documents and judging which sources are more likely to be correct. Also identify gaps in the story and decide how best to handle them.
- **Rewrite, edit and proofread.** Turning your initial timeline or draft into a ready-to-share narrative is going to take time and effort—use NaNoWriMo to your advantage. Consider joining a family history writing session at Family Tree University to guide you through this process.
- **Create a different kind of family story project.** Try framing ancestral photos with their accompanying stories; these make cherished gifts. You also could create an album with photos of relatives, family homes, or heirlooms. Another option is a professionally printed family tree chart or a personalized map of your DNA ethnicity, such as those from Family ChartMasters <familychartmasters.com>.

DECEMBER
Celebrate traditions

Take a break this month from serious ancestor hunting to enjoy time with living relatives. This doesn't mean you have to ignore family history. In fact, it's an ideal time to let your family heritage inspire your thoughts and activities.

- **Enrich seasonal celebrations with favorite family traditions.** Be open to reviving forgotten traditions or creating new ones based on your family heritage. Concoct old favorite recipes together; hang decorations; have a storytelling night or participate in faith-based rituals. Take care with new or outside-the-comfort-zone activities: When everyone comes together, stick with experiences everyone will enjoy.
- **Consider creating a display that honors relatives who've passed.** The holidays are difficult for many who're grieving or lonely for absent loved ones. You might purchase or create an ornament, wreath or other holiday décor item in someone's memory (search for memorial ornaments on Pinterest <www.pinterest.com> for inspiration). Before festivities begin, you could observe a moment of silence or light a candle in remembrance of loved ones. •

Contributing editor **Sunny Jane Morton** hopes to accomplish two tasks per month from these ideas. What's your goal for the new year?

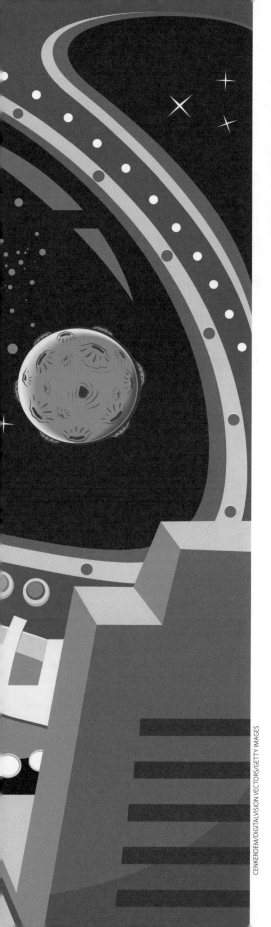

Make sure your stellar research log includes these six key pieces of information.

by KERRY SCOTT

Here's a confession; I love gadgets. If you've ever wondered who in the world needs all of these fancy tools to be productive, it's me. If it's shiny and needs to be charged, I probably want it. When I'm working on my genealogical research, though, my most useful tool doesn't have a cord, an extended warranty or a hefty price tag. The one tool I'd be lost without is my research log.

When I was a brand-new genealogist, more seasoned researchers told me I needed a log, and I scoffed. Then I spent years doing the same work over and over, because I wasn't keeping track of my efforts. Now I face far fewer brick walls because I'm able to move my research forward instead of going around in circles.

Research logs help you see what you've done, what you need to do and where to go next. If you take a break from your research for a few months (or years), you'll be able to pick up where you left off. These days, I never do any genealogical work without my research log.

HIGHLY LOGICAL

In the olden days (1995), my research log was on paper. With today's technological advances, I think a research log is more useful if it's electronic, but pen and paper are always an option. A computer-based research log is easy to find, and you can add to it forever. It doesn't waste paper or printer ink, and modern automatic backup systems and cloud-based storage can help ensure that it's available even if disaster strikes.

I use Evernote <www.evernote.com> because it's available on all of my gadgets and backs up in the cloud. However, even a Word document can be an effective research log. The platform isn't important; the discipline of recording *all* of your research is what matters most.

I encourage you to overcome the idea that a research log is too much work. Once you're past the learning curve of a new system, your log saves valuable time better spent breaking down your brick walls and finding new ancestors to add to your family tree.

1 DATE OF RESEARCH

Captain Obvious, you say? A lot of people don't realize how useful the date of research can be. New records are being digitized all the time, so assessing how long ago you looked for something and *didn't* find it can help determine when it's time to try again.

For example, my research logs from 2014 contained notes indicating that my ancestors' church records in Norway weren't available online. The date prompted me to try again, and I was rewarded with two generations' worth of new discoveries.

Dates can also help you spot patterns in your research cycle. You can choose when to subscribe to certain websites so you can pay for them when you'll actually use them. My research logs tell me I tend to work on my own family tree more in the summer, when hot weather keeps me indoors with the air-conditioning. So I can budget for genealogy website subscriptions in the summer months, when I'll get the most value for my dollars.

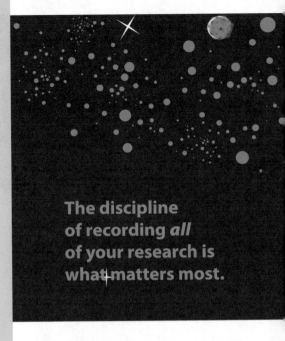

The discipline of recording *all* of your research is what matters most.

2 FULL SOURCE CITATIONS

I know—source citations aren't that much fun. You feel like they'll slow you down, and you promise you'll go back and do them later, right?

Odds are you won't. Do your future self a favor and create source citations right then and there. Doing so will prevent that awful feeling when you realize at the end of a research trip that you don't have a page number, author's name or other key detail. You'll also have everything ready for the day you write up your research conclusions (which increases the odds that you *will* do those write-ups).

I've also found that it's easier to learn how to do citations quickly and correctly if you do one every few minutes. The quick repetition really helps your brain to learn a new skill.

3 DETAILS, DETAILS, DETAILS

You think you'll remember that exciting record forever, but odds are you won't. When you've been working on your family trees for decades you'll be amazed at how quickly today's research details fade from memory. Beyond the basic outline of what you find in a particular document, what else will you record? Does a witness name ring a bell? Does the document spur new ideas? Put all of it in your research log. There's no such thing as too much information here.

If you've discovered a database or resource that might be handy later on, copy and paste the URL into your research log. By copying and pasting the URL you avoid introducing typos. That will allow you to come back to it with a single click.

4 KEYWORDS THAT RELATE TO THE SEARCH

Your research log's data is only useful if you can find it again. Many family historians struggle to find a digital filing system that works for them. Your filing system doesn't have to be perfect, and this is where adding keywords can really help.

If you're not yet sure of the spelling of a newly discovered ancestor's name, add all of the spellings you can think of to cover your bases. For example, if you're working on a woman whose maiden name is still a mystery, include text with her husband's name, the town she lived in or other identifying details. This will save you from having to wade through every "Mary" on your computer when you're looking for *this* Mary.

In some families, even full names aren't that helpful. I have German ancestors who reused the same names over and over. My Norwegian forebears were worse; they used patronyms, which changed each generation.

In order to keep them straight, I've developed nicknames, and I tag each research log entry with the nickname. This helps me not confuse *Milwaukee Fred* with *Railroad Fred* or *Dead Fred*. (Of course, they're all dead. But "Dead" Fred died very young, and had his name passed along to the next child—a common practice among Germans). I also have a string of *Nels Nelsons*, so *Civil War Nels* is labeled differently from *Norway Nels* (who lived in the Old Country) and *Minnesota Nels* (who was born in—you guessed it—Minnesota).

Some people use ancestor numbers assigned by their desktop genealogy software as unique keywords for each ancestor. Do whatever helps you find the right person.

5 EXPENSES

Your research log is a great place to keep track of costs when you send a request for a death certificate or pension file. Whether you're on a strict budget or not, it's smart to track your spending and to stay within bounds.

Recording those costs can also provide some accountability, so you don't accidentally go on a late night record-ordering spree and blow your budget for the year in one fell swoop. (I've done that, and I don't recommend it.) It's helpful to look back and see how much a particular record cost the last time you ordered, so you can better prioritize what to order next.

6 NOTES TO YOUR FUTURE SELF

If you're researching records in a particular area, you probably have an ancestor who lived there. And if you have one ancestor in an area, you'll probably find that you have more.

Consider what information might be useful to you when you have to return to this spot. Did you just learn that the county line moved in 1846? Put that in the log. Did the street numbering system change? Is the database on this obscure website you've found picky about having surnames capitalized for searching? Save your future self grief by making note of it all.

Kerry Scott organizes her genealogy from her home in Albuquerque, N.M. She authored the book *How to Use Evernote for Genealogy* (Family Tree Books).

Turn the page for an out-of-this-world research log template

Research Log Template

Send your research into warp speed by recording your searches, findings and notes in a log.

Date _____ **Task (include keywords used)** _____

Notes (include search summary, source citations) _____

_____

_____

_____

_____

Expenses _____

Date _____ **Task (include keywords used)** _____

Notes (include search summary, source citations) _____

_____

_____

_____

_____

Expenses _____

Date _____ **Task (include keywords used)** _____

Notes (include search summary, source citations) _____

_____

_____

_____

_____

Expenses _____

Date _____ **Task (include keywords used)** _____

Notes (include search summary, source citations) _____

_____

_____

_____

_____

Expenses _____

Date _____ **Task (include keywords used)** _____

Notes (include search summary, source citations) _____

_____

_____

_____

_____

Expenses _____

 Download typable versions of this and other useful genealogy forms at <www.familytreemagazine.com/freeforms/researchforms>.

Online Search Tracker

Collection Name: _____   Website: _____

Name

First and Middle Names	Last Name

Keywords

Events

	Date	Location
Birth		
Arrival		
Lived In		
Marriage		
Death		

Relationships

Relationship	First Name	Last Name

Collection Name: _____   Website: _____

Name

First and Middle Names	Last Name

Keywords

Events

	Date	Location
Birth		
Arrival		
Lived In		
Marriage		
Death		

Relationships

Relationship	First Name	Last Name

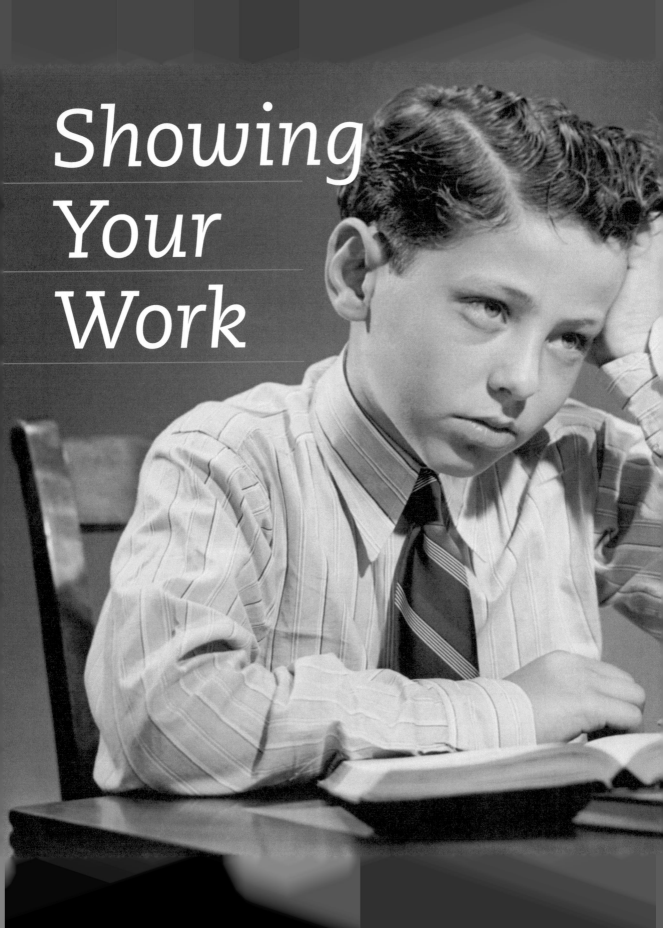

Showing Your Work

Though not glamorous, citing your sources can reap great rewards for your research. Here's how to start.

by ANDREW KOCH

Eating green vegetables. Flossing your teeth. Hitting the gym. These things are good for us, but that doesn't mean we're excited to do them.

To me, there's no clearer family history equivalent of finishing your broccoli than citing sources. Creating accurate source citations can be dull and take lots of time, and—though they might acknowledge the importance of doing so—many researchers are unsure how they should start.

The good news is that, with reference books and online tools, adequately citing sources has never been easier. Citation is built right into the most popular tree-building tools, from Ancestry.com's Member Trees <www.ancestry.com> to the RootsMagic desktop software <www.rootsmagic. com>. And services like EasyBib <www.easybib.com> can generate citations for you in a variety of styles.

Let's take a look at source citations: why you need them, what to include, and how to decide what format you should record them in.

WHY SOURCE CITATIONS

At a very basic level, source citations help someone viewing your research understand where you got your information. And you can cite all kinds of sources, from books to online records to interviews to emails.

In case you need some convincing, source citations will help your research by:

• **Adding credibility:** Source citations "show your work," demonstrating to others where you found information and how you reached your conclusions. This holds you accountable, disclosing your sources and allowing your readers to evaluate how reliable they are. This is particularly true if you're hoping to publish research, or are seeking credentials from a body like the Board for Certification of Genealogists (BCG).

• **Re-tracing information:** If you're ever questioned on a fact or need to resolve conflicting details, citations give you a quick path to revisiting your documents. This will save you valuable time, especially when you come back to research after an extended period.

• **Identifying new records:** By being intentional in documenting your sources, you'll begin to notice if you're overly reliant on one particular resource. This can be your invitation to seek out other resources to diversify your research, especially if (for example) you find you've

> **tip**
> When deciding how much detail to include in source citations, err on the side of too much. You can always strip out information depending on what style guide or format you're publishing in.

Sample Source Citations

Your source citations will vary based on type of record and what system you're using, but here are a few samples to get you started. The different colors indicate different types of information.

You can download a two-page chart listing what details to include in citations for various types of records at <www.familytreemagazine.com/freebie/free-genealogy-source-documentation-guide>.

Record type	Citation
Census return microfilm image, accessed online	1940 US Census, Washington, DC, population schedule, enumeration district 1-74, sheet 61a, entry for Franklin D. Roosevelt; digital image, Ancestry.com (ancestry.com/imageviewer/collections/2442/images/M-T0627-00555-00418: accessed 2 June 2021); citing National Archives and Records Administration microfilm T627, Washington, DC, 1940.
Death register microfilm image, accessed online	"Pennsylvania, Pittsburgh City Deaths, 1870–1905," microfilm 505841, DGS number 4672714, image 126 of 695, page 602, death register for Peter Joyce; digital image, FamilySearch (www.familysearch.org/ark:/61903/3:1:939V-8QSW-62; accessed 3 Jun 2021); citing Allegheny County Courthouse, Pittsburgh, Penn., 1888.
Photograph from online collection	"FDR [Franklin Delano Roosevelt]," glass negative, Harris & Ewing Collection, 1938; digital photograph, US Library of Congress Online Catalog, Harris & Ewing Collection (www.loc.gov/item/2016883801/; accessed 3 June 2021); held by Library of Congress Prints and Photographs Division, Washington, DC, call number LC-H21-C-820 [P&P].

KEY:
- Title/Description
- Location within Collection
- Year of Creation/Publication
- Format
- Website Access Information
- Physical Repository Information

only been using indexes and should seek out original records.

- **Giving credit where it's due:** Genealogy is all about collaboration. By referencing the websites, societies, archives, record collections, and fellow researchers who have helped you along the way, you're essentially saying "thanks"—plus acting as a referral to others.

- **Grounding your research:** Well-formatted source citations are the same no matter where you're working: online family trees, desktop software programs, or even a handwritten journal. As your work moves to new platforms or across multiple devices, your citations (if kept consistently) will help anchor your research.

The scholarly best practice is to cite any fact that isn't common knowledge. Everyone knows that George Washington was the first US president under the Constitution, so you don't need to cite a source when stating that. But how was

his estate, Mount Vernon, laid out? And who was Washington's next-in-command during the French and Indian War? Those details require research, and thus would need to be cited.

WHAT TO INCLUDE

The length and format of a source citation (including what details are in it) will vary based on the document or publication you're citing. A citation for a government-created record, for example, will look significantly different from one for a printed book.

As a result, it's crucial to study the source in question: where it comes from, when it was created and by whom, and how it's being accessed. In <www.familytreemagazine.com/organization/5-elements-source-citation> (based on the work of Thomas W. Jones), Shannon Combs-Bennett outlines the five basic details that a source citation should include, regardless of type of source:

Source citations "show your work," demonstrating to others where you found information and how you reached your conclusions.

1. *Who created the information* (e.g., an author, an editor, a transcriber or a government)

2. *What the source is*: the title (e.g., for a book) or a description of what kind of document the item is

3. *When the source was created and/or published*

4. *Where in the larger work the information is* (e.g., a page number)

5. *Where the source is* (i.e., where it is physically or online)

Let's look at an example. For a US passenger list, you'd want to include:

1. *Who*: the US Department of Labor Immigration Service (which created the original record) or the National Archives (which houses microfilms of the record)

2. *What*: a passenger arrival list, with a note about what format the list was viewed in

3. *When*: the year the immigration took place

4. *Where in*: the location of the list within the larger collection (e.g., the date, if the collection is organized chronologically), plus line number

5. *Where at*: the name of the archive that holds the record (in this case, the National Archives and Records Administration), plus where you accessed the image

Note that last piece: In addition to *type* of source, your citations will also document *how you accessed it*—the format in which you viewed the source. So a citation for a passenger list will look different if you requested a copy from the National Archives versus viewing a microfilm at a library versus finding an image on FamilySearch <www.familysearch.org>.

Check out an in-depth tutorial for citing sources using popular family tree-builders <www.familytreemagazine.com/organization/genealogy-software-source-citations>.

In other words, if you viewed a digital image of a microfilmed passenger list on FamilySearch, you'd want to include information about the digital source *as well as* the physical source used to create it: what format the record was in, the website's URL, and when you accessed it.

You might make additional notes to clarify how the digital source came to be. For example, many of the National Archives' records have been digitized or otherwise made available by FamilySearch or commercial sites like Ancestry.com <www.ancestry.com>.

So the full source citation for a passenger list image viewed on FamilySearch might look like this:

"New York Passenger Arrival List (Ellis Island), 1892–1924," roll 2945, volume 6740–6741, *S.S. Rotterdam*, 2 April 1921, line 8 (entry for Albert Einstein); digital image, FamilySearch (www.familysearch.org/ark:/61903/3:1:3Q9M-C95R-49LQ-T: accessed 3 June 2021); citing National Archives and Records Administration microfilm T715, Washington, DC.

As you can see, making a citation requires you to learn quite a bit about where a source comes from. We've included a few more samples in the sidebar on page 36.

HOW TO FORMAT

You may feel anxious approaching source citations because you don't know what format to put them in. But take some solace in the fact that there is no *single* citation system that will work for all sources in all situations, nor one that should be used by all researchers.

You can certainly take advantage of tried-and-true templates. Elizabeth Shown Mills' 892-page

tip

Don't settle for the collection descriptions on sites like Ancestry.com and FamilySearch. These are generally not consistent from one collection to the next, nor do they have all the details needed for a proper citation. Take the information *from* them and apply to your own system instead.

tome *Evidence Explained: History Sources from Artifacts to Cyberspace* (Genealogical Publishing Co.) is widely considered the gold standard of genealogy source citation, with samples for just about every resource you can think of. (Mills has great resources on her website, too <www.evidenceexplained.com>.) Some publications or organizations will have their own style guides, such as the BCG *Genealogy Standards* or the Notes and Bibliography (NB) System of the Chicago Manual of Style.

Types of Citations

Another factor to consider when developing your citation template: where you'll be including citations, be it in research logs, online family trees, narrative histories, books or even on paper copies of records themselves. The length and format will be dictated, in part, on how much space you have, and how you'll be documenting sources in relation to the rest of the work (e.g., if you're writing a narrative and want to cite sources in the text as you go).

In general, source-documentation will take one of three forms: in-text citations, footnotes/endnotes, or a bibliography.

● **In-text**, or parenthetical, citations are used to cite the source for a fact within the narrative of written projects. A citation (usually in some abbreviated format) is indicated in parentheses after the associated fact. A longer citation is generally included at the end of the work in a bibliography (see below).

● **Footnotes** or **endnotes** also refer the reader to a source from within text, but via a superscript[1] and to a citation somewhere else in the document. At the bottom of the page (in the footnote) or at the end of the document (in the endnote), you cite your source in full. If you reference the same source again within a project, you may not need to include the full citation; many style guides allow for abbreviated citations upon second (and further) reference. This is considered the most thorough method, since it allows you to link full citation directly to facts.

● A **source list** (or **bibliography**) simply compiles all your sources in one place, usually sorting them alphabetically by author or title. Each listing in a bibliography will closely resemble the first-reference footnote/endnote citation, but there may be differences in how information is organized.

---

[1] The small number indicates either a footnote (at the bottom of the page) or an end note (at the end of a document). For the purposes of in-text source citations, this is where you'd add your citation entry.

But having said that, most genealogists can develop a system that suits their own needs. In fact, your source citation is effective as long as someone reviewing your research can successfully identify where you got your information.

Here are some quick tips for making your own source-citation system:

● Create a document that explains your system and includes examples. Note-taking services like Evernote <www.evernote.com> or word-processing programs like Google Docs <docs.google.com> can help.

● Use punctuation to separate items. Most systems call for commas or semicolons between data points, plus a period at the end.

● Create templates, especially for commonly used sources. This will help you quickly create consistent citations. (For example: Do you *always* include the full URL for a web-based source, or just the URL for the collection's page?)

● Determine where you'd like to include citations. Do you have plans to publish your work? If so, make sure your system complies with the publication's style guide or an industry standard like the Genealogical Proof Standard (GPS).

● Try to anticipate special cases. Prepare for scenarios where you'll need to cite (for example) a whole family's record instead of just one person's entry.

● Anticipate missing information. Not all sources will have all the details you expect, so determine how you'll handle situations in which you don't have details like an author name or a page number.

● Borrow from existing systems. You don't need to reinvent the wheel, so consider adapting standard styles for your own use rather than trying to build from scratch. Elizabeth Shown Mills outlines her system in *Evidence Explained* and in abbreviated form in *Evidence!* (both Genealogical Publishing Co.). It's based in the Chicago Manual of Style.

So, editor's orders: Make source citations as you go. They won't help you lose weight, build strong bones, or prevent gingivitis, but they might just save you some heartache. ●

Andrew Koch is the editor of *Family Tree Magazine*. Many moons ago as a writing tutor in college, he had to learn source-citation templates for multiple manuals of style.

Genealogy Source List

Use this list to fully document sources you've referenced in your research.

SOURCE NO.	CITATION

TIES that BIND

Organize your research for easy travel and sharing by creating family history binders. Here's how to get started.

by THE EDITORS OF FAMILY TREE MAGAZINE

Dog people versus cat people, team Mac versus team PC, even how to put toilet paper on the roll (in front of or behind)—no matter the subject, people will find ways of dividing themselves. And genealogists are no exception, getting drawn into a feud with just as much passion: whether to organize research into binders, or folders.

Folders certainly have their advantages, and we've covered filing systems based on folders <www.familytreemagazine.com/organization/5-genealogy-filing-systems>. But organizing research in binders makes it easier to transport and share with others, particularly those who might be newer to family history.

Of course, the binder-versus-folder debate is not a zero-sum game: You can use both types of storage. Perhaps you store your research in folders, but prepare a binder for a specific purpose such as sharing research or handing information over to a client. You could also use *neither* binders nor folders, preferring to keep your system 100% digital.

We're not here to take sides. But we do want to share some guidance on how to put together a family history research binder. These six simple steps will get you started.

1 GATHER YOUR SUPPLIES

The first thing to consider is what kind of binder you want to use. If your binder is meant to be passed around and shared, you may want to opt for more durable materials. But if you intend to store and archive your binder, you should consider using archival-grade materials that are less likely to deteriorate on their own.

Because of this, the amount and type of materials you will need depend on the goal and scale of your specific project. So you'll need to determine how you'll be using the binder, where it will be stored, and how large you'd like it to be before buying supplies.

Here's a basic list of what all you'll need to begin your project:

- 3-ring binder
- Document sleeves or sheet protectors
- Tabs or dividers
- Blank paper or family tree templates and/or printouts of research
- Photos

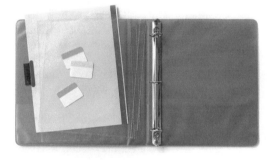

2 CHOOSE YOUR ORGANIZATIONAL METHOD

This is the trickiest part! The best organizational method will depend on your goal and family structure. But here are five filing systems we recommend in <www.familytreemagazine.com/organization/5-genealogy-filing-systems>:

- **Ancestral:** This basic filing system organizes around a single family, beginning with one individual and including records of all his ancestors through a certain number of generations. Each binder begins with a pedigree chart, then is followed by a section for each ancestor (organized by birth date and/or generation) in that chart, along with accompanying records.

- **Married Couple:** This system focuses on family units, with each binder (or, for smaller families, subsections within a binder) documenting a married couple and their descendants. You'll begin with a family group sheet or descendant report. Subsections are organized by ancestor.
- **Surname:** If you're still in the thick of your research, you might want a system more flexible to new discoveries. In this method, each binder covers a surname—regardless of what family unit the individual came from. Subsections are for record type, rather than specific ancestor, so you might label sections *SMITH: Birth*, then *SMITH: Census*, and so on. (Note: File records for married women by their maiden names, as that's how they'll appear in reports and charts.)
- **Geographic:** Each binder has a dedicated region or state, with records sorted by surname or subject. You can further subdivide by record group, or include sections for separate counties or provinces. This is useful if you're sampling a few records from multiple places or documents that cover wide areas.
- **Record Type:** Place all documents of a particular kind in one binder, with subsections for surname or other identifiers (such as record year). This can be useful for documents like censuses that contain several people. Create a catchall binder for unusual resources, such as oral history interview transcripts, letters from modern relatives, or a relative's memoir.

You can also mix-and-match your binder methods. For example, if you wanted to document the ancestors of John Smith, you could create a binder for him that begins with his records, then has separate sections for each of his ancestors (his father, mother, paternal grandfather, paternal grandmother, maternal grandfather, maternal grandmother, and so on).

But what to do with census records, which will likely mention multiple members of the family? You could create a separate binder that collects one kind of record—censuses—and sort it by year or place. Then you could include references to that binder in your Smith family binder. (For example: "The Robert and Mary Smith census record for 1930 appears on page 5 of the binder titled *Springfield Census Records*.")

Note: For simplicity's sake, the rest of the article will follow how to create a binder using that first Ancestral method, but many of the principles will apply to other systems as well.

③ FILL OUT A PEDIGREE CHART

Knowing which ancestors to include in your binder is an important step, as it will give an outline to your project and (in the Ancestral method) will serve as a kind of "table of contents" for your binder. Using a templated five-generation ancestor chart (like the one we have for free at <www.familytreemagazine.com/freebie/five generationancestorchart>) will help.

In her book *Family History 101* (Family Tree Books), author Marcia Melnyk shares a few tips for how to fill out a pedigree chart:

- **Write surnames in capital letters:** The all-caps approach lets you (or someone reading your charts) immediately distinguish last names from first and middle names.
- **If you know middle names, spell them out:** Naturally, this helps you distinguish Grandpa William *Randolph* Reynolds from Grandpa William *Robert* Reynolds.
- **Always record nicknames,** denoting them in quotations. You want to show your ancestors' full identities, so you can match up family history to the right relative.
- **List women's maiden names,** not their married names. Since you're recording your female ancestors right next to their husbands, including their married names is redundant.

 Find a downloadable version of this guide at <www.familytreemagazine.com/freebie/how-to-make-a-family-history-binder-printable-guide>.

Sample Binder Organization

Say you want to create a binder that tracks five generations of John Smith's family, from him to his great-great-grandparents. Here's how you might outline that binder:

Title Page

\>

"Letter from the editor"
explaining the binder's scope, as well as any research that still needs to be completed

\>

Five-generation ancestor chart
of the Smith family, with John Smith on far left

\>

**Person 1:
John Smith record summary**

- Birth and/or baptismal certificate (or index)
- Marriage certificate or bans
- Census records
- (and so on)

\>

**Person 2:
John Smith's father**

- Birth and/or baptismal certificate (or index)
- Marriage certificate or bans
- Census records
- (and so on)

\>

**Person 3:
John Smith's mother**

- Birth and/or baptismal certificate (or index)
- Marriage certificate or bans
- Census records
- (and so on)

\>

**Person 4:
John Smith's paternal grandfather**

- Birth and/or baptismal certificate (or index)
- Marriage certificate or bans
- Census records
- (and so on)

\>

**Sections for
Persons 5 through 31**

\>

Appendix

- Maps
- Timeline (including any immigration dates, border changes, etc.)

- **Format dates as *day, month, full year*.** For consistency, genealogists usually write dates in the "European" style, flipflopping the American convention of *month, day, year*. So, for example, the day the Declaration of Independence was ratified should be written as *4 JUL 1776* rather than *July 4, 1776* or *7/4/1776*. Notice, also, the use of the abbreviated, all-caps month rather than a numeral.

4 CREATE SECTION OPENERS

After you've completed your pedigree chart, it's time to outline for the rest of your binder. For our example, that means building out sections for individual ancestors.

You might find it helpful to begin each ancestor's section with some sort of fact sheet or biography. Make sure to include the person's birth, marriage and death dates; any known residences; names and birth dates of any children; and other genealogically relevant details that might generate records (e.g., occupation or military service). You'll want to make sure you're consistent in how you begin each section.

We have an Ancestor Research Worksheet that includes many of the needed introductory details in a quick, at-a-glance format <www.familytreemagazine.com/freebie/researchworksheet>. Other options include a short narrative summary of the person's life, or even a family group sheet.

5 ADD AND TRACK RECORDS

Once you've gathered facts and biographical information for each ancestor, it's time to create a personal record inventory. This is a detailed list of each kind of record you've found for an ancestor, from birth to death.

After this summary, add photocopies of any and all of those records, in chronological order. You can three-hole-punch them if more convenient, but make sure not to punch out any details. (And remember that any original

> When organizing your binder, you may find that a system for numbering your ancestors will come in handy. Drew Smith explores some options in <www.familytreemagazine.com/organization/genealogy-numbering-systems>.

materials should be placed in archival-safe page protectors.) Avoid stapling or gluing materials together, as this will make it more difficult to turn pages—and potentially damage items. Add a note indicating where the original record (if available) is stored.

For oversized or fragile documents, keep copies in a binder and originals in separate archival storage. Save space and supplies by filing multiple-page (or otherwise related) documents in the same sheet protector. But don't file fragile originals or materials of different types (such as photos and newsprint) together.

Once you've created your first section, repeat steps 4 and 5 for each ancestor in your pedigree chart. Having a consistent structure within each section will make it easier to quickly find materials.

6 ASSEMBLE YOUR BINDER

Time to put it all together! Remember to label the binder's spine with the appropriate surname, and label tabbed dividers for easy reference.

Here are a few other ideas for additional sections and elements you can include:
- a "note from the editor" to explain the scope of your research
- a notes page (either within each section for details that don't fit nicely into a records inventory, or at the end of the binder for future discoveries)
- a dedicated photos section (useful if photos have multiple ancestors in them)
- maps
- timelines or other information about the time and period the family lived

And there you have it! Now you can proudly show off your completed project at the next holiday gathering or family reunion. ●

Table of Contents: Research Binder
Record your binder's layout.

Subject: _____

Compiled by: _____

Section no.	Section title	Section contents	Notes

Work It Out

Census Checklist
Follow ancestors and their famili...
Document whi...

Ancestor Worksheet
...one place all the information you have about a person in your family tr...
...Women).

...ve-Generation Ancestor Chart
...the most famous format for family trees, this chart allows you ...
...ltiple generations of an individual's direct-line ...

...ily Group Sheet
...parents, children and subsequent spouses) in detail.

Keep your research
in order with these
top-of-the line
genealogy worksheets.

by THE EDITORS OF FAMILY TREE MAGAZINE

Even the best-laid plans of mice, men and genealogists can go awry without an organized way of documenting your research.

These seven worksheets will keep your research on track and in order. We've provided tips and tricks for using each. Write directly in the magazine, or make a photocopy.

You can find more great, downloadable genealogy worksheets on our website <www.familytreemagazine.com/freeforms>.

- **Family Group Sheet**
- **Five-Generation Ancestor Chart**
- **Ancestor Worksheet**
- **Surname Variant Chart**
- **Oral History Interview Record**
- **Census Checklist**
- **Passenger List Search Worksheet**

AL PARRISH

Family Group Sheet

Look at one family unit (parents, children and subsequent spouses) in detail.

The _____ Family

Husband

Source #

Include cross-references to records so you can easily source data.

Full Name _____ _____

Birth Date _____ Place _____ _____

Marriage Date _____ Place _____ _____

Death Date _____ Place _____ _____

    Burial _____ _____ _____

His Father _____ _____

His Mother with Maiden Name _____ _____

Wife

Full Name _____ _____

Birth Date _____ Place _____ _____

Death Date _____ Place _____ _____

    Burial _____ _____ _____

Her Father _____ _____

Her Mother with Maiden Name _____ _____

Other Spouses

Full Name _____ _____

    Marriage Date and Place _____ _____

Full Name _____ _____

    Marriage Date and Place _____ _____

Make a note if you've also created a Family Group Sheet for this couple's children.

Children of This Marriage	Birth Date and Place	Death and Burial Dates and Places	Spouse and Marriage Date and Place

Five-Generation Ancestor Chart

Perhaps the most famous format for family trees, this chart allows you
to view multiple generations of an individual's direct-line ancestors at once.

> Learn how to chart adoptive families, step-
> families and other "non-traditional" family
> arrangements <www.familytreemagazine.
> com/premium/genealogy-chart-faqs>.

4

birth date and place

marriage date and place

death date and place

2

birth date and place

marriage date and place

death date and place

5

birth date and place

death date and place

1

birth date and place

marriage date and place

death date and place

spouse

3

birth date and place

death date and place

6

birth date and place

marriage date and place

death date and place

7

birth date and place

death date and place

tip You'll recognize this chart as one of
the default views from online family
trees. It's called the "Pedigree" view at
Ancestry.com and MyHeritage, and the
"Landscape" view on FamilySearch.org.

Label your five-generation ancestor charts to help you keep track of this frequently used worksheet.

Chart # ___

1 on this chart = ___ on chart # ___

16

see chart #

8

birth date and place

17

marriage date and place

death date and place

18

9

19

birth date and place

death date and place

20

10

21

birth date and place

marriage date and place

death date and place

22

11

23

birth date and place

death date and place

24

12

25

birth date and place

marriage date and place

death date and place

26

13

27

birth date and place

death date and place

28

14

29

birth date and place

marriage date and place

death date and place

30

15

31

birth date and place

death date and place

Make a note about what other five-generation ancestor charts are associated with each ancestor. Then, you can link charts to create a chain that stretches back even further.

Ancestor Worksheet

Record in one place all the information you have about a person in your family tree.

Full Name (Maiden Name for Women): _____

Social Security Number: _____

Nicknames and Alternate Names: _____

Surname Spelling Variations: _____

Track spelling variations in the Surname Variant Chart.

Birth and Baptism

Birth Date: _____   Birth Place: _____

Baptism Date: _____   Baptism Place: _____

Marriage(s) and Divorce(s)

Name of Spouse(s)	Marriage Date(s)	Marriage Place(s)

Name of Spouse(s)	Divorce Date(s)	Divorce Place(s)

Death

Death Date: _____   Death Place: _____

Burial Date: _____   Burial Church/Place: _____

Obituary Date(s) and Newspaper(s): _____

Military Service

Conflict (if applicable)	Unit	Dates/Years

Migration

You can track more details of your ancestor's travels in the Passenger List Search Worksheet.

From	To	Departure/ Arrival Dates	Companion(s)	Ship (if applicable)

Personal Information

Schools Attended: _____

Religion/Church(es) Attended: _____

Hobbies/Club/Memberships: _____

Children

Your ancestors' hobbies may seem insignificant compared to their other life details. But this information can flesh out your research and lead you to records, such as those kept by fraternal organizations.

Child's Name	Birth Date	Birthplace	Other Parent

Use this field to indicate which spouse he or she had this child with, or if the ancestor you're studying had a child with someone other than his or her spouse.

Friends, Witnesses, and Neighbors to Research

Name	Relationship

Surname Variant Chart

Keep track of your ancestral surnames, plus the different ways
you've found them spelled in records and record indexes.

Surname			
Place of Origin			
Phonetic Variants			
Possible Variations into English			
Surname Suffixes (*-son, -datter, etc.*)			
Other Spellings/ Variants			

Names weren't changed at Ellis Island, but they may have been misheard by a non-native speaker at your ancestor's point of departure. Use this field to track some possible ways a surname may have been misheard and misspelled.

 An unusual last name may actually be a blessing. David A. Fryxell shares six tips for researching ancestors who have atypical surnames <www.familytreemagazine.com/premium/unusual-last-names>.

Oral History Interview Record

Log who you interviewed, when the interview took place and what became of the interview's recording.

Interview Date: _____   Interview Place: _____

Name of Interviewer: _____   Relationship to Interviewee: _____

Name of Interviewee: _____   Other Names: _____

Recording Format: _____   Recording Location: _____

Notes from the Interview

_____
_____
_____
_____
_____
_____
_____
_____
_____
_____
_____
_____
_____
_____
_____
_____
_____
_____
_____
_____
_____
_____

tip Fill out an Ancestor Worksheet for the person you're interviewing, both before and during the interview. This will help you identify details you need to ask about. For more interview tips (including questions you should ask), see <www.familytreemagazine.com/premium/20-questions>.

Census Checklist

Follow ancestors and their families through the decades.
Document which US federal censuses you've found them in.

Ancestor Name	1790	1800	1810	1820	1830	1840	1850	1860	1870	1880	1900	1910	1920	1930	1940	1950

tip You may notice we omitted the 1890 federal census from this chart. Sadly, this wasn't a mistake. Two fires destroyed most records from the 1890 census. Learn more about the disasters and what substitutes you should consult <www.familytreemagazine.com/ premium/holes-history-1890-census-fire>.

Obviously, none of your ancestors appeared in all 16 surviving US federal censuses. Note which censuses didn't occur in your ancestor's lifetime, and make a hashmark or write *n/a* in the appropriate columns.

Passenger List Search Worksheet

Keep your ancestor's departure and arrival information handy.

Migration Information

Estimate Departure Date: _____ From Which Country/Region? _____

Possible Departure Ports: _____

Ship Name: _____ Age at Immigration: _____

Estimated Arrival Date: _____

Possible Arrival Ports: _____

Possible Traveling Companions

Name	Sex	Age

Study the history of your ancestor's homeland to determine what country it may have been part of during his/her lifetime.

Sources to Check

Source or Database	Repository or Website	Date Searched

tip

Use this template in conjunction with the Ancestor Worksheet. When researching passenger lists, you'll need to reference your immigrant ancestor's name, birth date and birthplace, as well as information about his or her spouse and children.

Your-Digital-Files.jpg

Clean up your computer with this guide to managing and labeling digital files.

by RICK CRUME

I f you do much family history research, you've probably accumulated hundreds—maybe even thousands—of digital files: historical records, excerpts from books you have found online, scanned family photographs and pictures of gravestones made with a digital camera. With all that data, keeping your digital files organized can feel like an overwhelming task.

You need a standard system for organizing those records—plus some way to label photographs with names, dates and places. You also need to be able to find a particular record or photograph when you need it. Read on for tips and tools that will help bring order to all the family history files on your computer.

ADD CUSTOM NAMES TO ELECTRONIC FILES.

When you scan a photograph or find a historical record online, save the file to your computer with a descriptive name. The default names generated for most files (e.g., "IMG_0001") won't be meaningful to your research or help you find the file later. Instead, take some time to create custom file names.

While really long file names can become unwieldy, you should include enough information so you can see—at a glance—what the file is. You'll also need to be mindful of your device's character limits—file names in Windows 10, for example, can only be 260 characters long.

But you don't just want your file names to be descriptive—you also want them to be consistent. Create a standard file-naming system so your files are listed in an order that's useful for your purposes. For example, you could name files:

- **By surname**: This makes it easy to jump to files pertaining to a particular branch of your family or to a specific person.

While really long file names can become unwieldy, you should include enough information so you can see—at a glance—what the file is.

- **By place**: If you have records that cover various surnames in the same localities, you might find it easier to label/sort your files by locale. Be consistent in how you indicate places—for example, use either full state names or abbreviations.
- **By date**: I'm writing a biography of a relative and it's helpful to have all my sources, including many newspaper articles, in chronological order.

When naming files, use *just* letters, numbers, hyphens and underscores. Don't use spaces, periods, parentheses, brackets or special characters, such as !, & or #. (Not all programs and devices can process files with these characters in their names.)

 Organize your files—both paper and digital—with these nine habits <www.familytreemagazine.com/organization/9-habits-of-highly-organized-genealogists>.

Here, newspaper articles are named in such a way that they're sorted chronologically by date of publication.

1900-12-09-MA-Boston-Herald-Page-13-GenealogyBank
1901-04-26-NY-Rome-Daily-Sentinel-Page-4-Old-Fulton-NY-Post-Cards
1901-04-26-NY-Troy-Times-Page-2-GenealogyBank
1901-04-26-NY-Watertown-Daily-Times-Page-2-GenealogyBank
1901-04-27-NJ-Trenton-Evening-Times-Page-7-GenealogyBank
1901-04-27-PA-Lebanon-Daily-News-Page-2-Newspapers-com
1901-04-28-PA-Philadelphia-Inquirer-Page-11-GenealogyBank
1901-05-01-NY-Hornell-Evening-Tribune-Page-1-GenealogyBank
1901-05-19-NJ-Trenton-Evening-Times-Page-1-GenealogyBank
1901-05-24-NY-Troy-Times-Page-2-GenealogyBank
1901-06-25-NY-Troy-Times-Page-3-GenealogyBank
1901-08-17-NY-Watertown-Daily-Times-Page-8-GenealogyBank
1901-09-21-NY-Watertown-Daily-Times-Page-12-GenealogyBank
1901-09-28-NY-Watertown-Daily-Times-Page-14-GenealogyBank
1902-01-11-NY-Nornell-Evening-Tribune-Page-1-GenealogyBank
1902-02-07-NY-Amsterdam-Daily-Democrat-Page-8- Old-Fulton-NY-Post-Cards
1903-06-17-NY-Amsterdam-Evening-Recorder-Page-5-Old-Fulton-NY-Post-Cards
1903-08-15-NY-Utica-Herald-Dispatch-Page-4-Old-Fulton-NY-Post-Cards
1903-12-19-NY-Amsterdam-Evening-Recorder-Page-7-Old-Fulton-NY-Post-Cards
1903-12-19-NY-Gloversville-Daily-Leader-page-9-Old-Fulton-NY-Post-Cards
1903-12-19-NY-New-York-Sun-Page-6-Newspapers-com
1903-12-20-DC-Washington-Times-Page-14-Newspapers-com
1903-12-29-NY-Gloversville-Daily-Leader-Page-9-NYSHistoricNewspapers-org
1905-Date-Unclear-NY-Syracuse-Herald-Page-Unknown-Old-Fulton-NY-Post-Cards

ORGANIZE FILES INTO FOLDERS.
Properly labeled folders can also help you organize your files. For example, you could have a folder called *Genealogy* and, within it, folders for surnames. Then, if you have a lot of files for one specific surname, you could create subfolders for different places, such as *IL Cook* for Cook County, Illinois. You could even add another level for record types, such as newspapers and vital records. I also have a folder for Genealogy Research Plans.

The same can apply to photos. Within my Pictures folder, I put photos from my digital camera in folders arranged by date, while old scanned photos go in surname folders.

USE GENEALOGY SOFTWARE AND ONLINE FAMILY TREES.
Whether you use genealogy software (like Family Tree Maker <www.mackiev.com/ftm> or RootsMagic <www.rootsmagic.com>) or an online family tree on Ancestry.com <www.ancestry.com>, FamilySearch <www.familysearch.org>, Findmypast <www.findmypast.com> or MyHeritage <www.myheritage.com>, you can attach scanned records and photos to individuals in your family tree. This gives you another opportunity to organize your digital files.

Using these programs, you can generally label a media item with a:

- **Title/caption**: You can briefly give the name, date and place, like *John Smith and Elizabeth Jones, wedding, 1921, Chicago*.
- **Date**: Standard dates include approximate (*abt 1921*), exact (*20 May 1921*), just a month and year (*May 1921*), or just a year (*1921*). Make sure you select a consistent format for full dates, such as DD MMM YYYY (e.g., *10 Jan 2020*).
- **Place**: Enter a town/township, county, state and country (*Chicago, Cook, Illinois, United States*), or just the county/state or state/country if you can't be more specific. Most genealogy software and online family trees prompt you to enter a standardized place name appropriate for the time period. Those place names usually include the country (e.g., United States or USA), along with the town/township, county and state.
- **Description**: Here you can include more details, such as a specific place. Describe the original photo (e.g., *tintype*, *carte de visite* or

Using and Transferring Metadata in Digital Photos

Metadata can help you store and transfer key details about files. But how can you edit metadata, and what happens to it when you move files between programs? To view or edit a photo's metadata, right-click on the file in Windows Explorer, then click on Properties and the Details tab. (In Photos for Mac, right-click an image and select Get Info.) You can search your digital files for words in the metadata, such as a name or a place.

There are two kinds of metadata that are relevant to digital preservation:

- **EXIF** (Exchangeable Image File) data is captured by your camera, phone or scanner. It includes date, location, camera settings and the type and size of the image file.
- **IPTC** (International Press Telecommunications Council) data, such as a caption and descriptive tags (keywords), can be added by users. Adobe <www.adobe.com>, the maker of Photoshop and Photoshop Elements software, incorporated IPTC into its XMP metadata standard.

We'll focus on IPTC data, which can be extremely useful for savvy archivists. According to Ken Watson, whose website All About Digital Photos <www.rideau-info.com/photos> has helpful information on working with digital images, IPTC standards can help future-proof your metadata. That data becomes *part* of the digital photo, contained inside the file and preserved for future software programs.

"[IPTC] is an internationally recognized standard, so your IPTC/XMP data will be viewable by someone 50 or 100 years from now," Watson writes. "The same cannot be said for programs that use some proprietary labelling schemes."

To put it another way: If you use photo software that abides by the IPTC/XMP standard, your labels and descriptive tags (keywords) should be readable by other programs that also follow the standard. For a list of photo software that supports IPTC Photo Metadata, go to <www.iptc.org/standards/photo-metadata/software-support>.

This is important to keep in mind if you need to switch programs or a company closes. For example, Google discontinued its popular Picasa photo software in 2014 and replaced it with Google Photos <www.google.com/photos>, an online application that has similar functionality but doesn't properly support IPTC/XMP.

As such, you might be hesitant to make the switch from Picasa to Google Photos. Fortunately (at time of writing) you can continue to use Picasa as long as it works with future updates of your operating system. And since Picasa generally follows the IPTC/XMP standard, labels and descriptive tags created with the program should be readable by other programs that comply with that standard. Since Google Photos doesn't support the IPTC standard, you'll want to transfer to a different program when the time comes.

Likewise, Microsoft <www.microsoft.com> ended support for its popular photo software, Windows (Live) Photo Gallery, in 2017, and replaced it with the Photos app included in Windows 10. Photo Gallery supports the XMP standard, but the Photos app doesn't. So I'll need to find a different program to support my tags and labels from Photo Gallery once that program stops working with future Windows updates.

Metadata doesn't always stay with a file on online family tree services or social networking sites. FamilySearch and Google Photos are good options because they preserve metadata, but you'll want to be careful as you upload and download images to and from others:

- **FamilySearch**: I uploaded a TIF photo to FamilySearch Memories and linked it to the Family Tree. When I downloaded the file, it was retained the type and size, along with the caption, descriptive tags and face tags.
- **Ancestry.com**: When I did the same at Ancestry.com and downloaded the picture from a Member Tree, the image was converted from TIF to JPG and lost its name data. The file name was also changed, reflecting the title I gave the photo within Ancestry.com.
- **MyHeritage**: Doing the same thing on MyHeritage, my TIF file was converted to JPG, but it kept the caption, descriptive tags and face tags.
- **Facebook**: When I downloaded photos that I had added to Facebook, file names were changed and metadata lost.
- **Google Photos**: Google preserves file name and metadata. Keeping original quality for your photos may require you to exceed your free storage limit.

This is an example of a photo with a visual label.

The brothers Jay Luther Crume (1896-1919) and Frank Miles Crume (1894-1983) dressed up for a Wild West photo. Probably taken between about 1909 and 1911 in Moorhead, Minnesota. This photo is in the possession of Rick Crume in 2020.

cabinet card) and, optionally, give its dimensions. You could also give the name and address of the person, record office or archive that has the original document or photo, plus the photographer's name and address. If you found the file online, give the website address.

Some websites provide additional options to describe media. On Ancestry.com, you can indicate the media type, such as portrait, document or headstone. On MyHeritage, you can add keywords. FamilySearch now lets you add topic tags to photos and documents, making them easier to search.

Likewise, you can label and tag photos on Facebook <www.facebook.com>, the popular social networking site. Google Photos <photos.google.com>, a free photo-sharing and storage service, automatically tags faces (though it misses some of them) and you can add a date, a place and a description.

Some media labels may be lost in a GEDCOM transfer. However, when you use RootsMagic's TreeShare feature or Family Tree Maker's FamilySync technology to synchronize the family file on your computer with an Ancestry Member Tree, media labels are successfully copied between your trees.

ADD VISUAL LABELS.

Another labeling option is to add text directly on a digital image, creating a visual label that can easily be seen without having to view the file's metadata. (See the next section and the sidebar for tips on working with metadata).

One way to create a visual label is to add a caption in white space below the photo. For instructions on how to manually add labels using various software programs, see Ken Watson's "Visible Captioning of Digital Photos" <www.rideau-info.com/photos/genealogy-captioning.html>.

Make a copy of your digital photo or document before making alterations (such as adding labels or captions) to it. You want to preserve a version of the original document—particularly if you no longer have access to the physical source.

USE METADATA TO LABEL DIGITAL PHOTOS.

More tech-savvy genealogists can make use of metadata, information about a file that's embedded within its coding. Though not immediately visible to users, metadata can contain details about a document's origin, contents and

The Limits of Face-Tagging

Many photo applications use facial-recognition tools to tag faces automatically (in addition to letting you manually tag faces). Face tags make it easy to search for photos of people, but they are not part of the IPTC standard. Programs use various proprietary systems to tag faces, and so often aren't compatible with each other. So, when labeling digital photos, you should include people's names in the title or caption and the description, not just in face tags.

If you've tagged photos in one program but are switching to another, a tool called Tag That Photo <www.tagthatphoto.com> can convert your tags and labels. It costs $49 per year, but you need only a one-year subscription if you convert all your tags at once. If you keep your subscription, you can continue using Tag That Photo's face-recognition technology to tag and index new photos as they're added to your library.

Sample File-Naming Templates

You can adapt your file names for different types of records, but generally try to keep a consistent system so you can easily find a particular file. In these three templates, I use hyphens within the name, date or place and underscores between those three parts. But you might find it more convenient to use hyphens throughout the file name.

NAME FIRST

surname-firstname_yyyy-mm-dd_state-place_event**.ext**

*Grant-Alva-A_1921-08-24_MN-Clay-County_Probate***.pdf**

Note: You could omit the word *County*.

PLACE FIRST

state-county-place_event_surname-firstname_yyyy-mm-dd**.ext.**

*ME-Aroostook-County_Deed-Index_Pennington_1808-1879_FHL-Film-10432***.pdf**

Note: Here, *FHL-Film* refers to a Family History Library microfilm.

DATE FIRST

yyyy-mm-dd_surname-firstname_ state-place_source**.ext**

*1903-08-13_KY-Lexington_Morning-Herald-Page-1_GenealogyBank***.pdf**

Note: This file is in a folder all pertaining to the same person, so I didn't include the person's name in the file name.

---

subjects—provided, of course, that another user can decode it.

To improve the chances that someone will be able to interpret your metadata, you'll want to follow certain standard guidelines that make metadata compatible with a wider variety of programs. See the sidebar for more details.

MANAGE PDFS.

Don't forget to update file names and metadata on your PDFs as well! You can edit a PDF's metadata in Adobe Acrobat or Adobe Acrobat Reader: File > Properties > Description tab (where you can add a title, author, subject and keywords).

When I link a document (such as a letter, diary or Civil War pension file) to a person in my genealogy software or online family tree, I scan the pages, then combine them into a single PDF. Even though the software or online family tree lets me add a title/caption, date, place and description, I like to include that information in

For more file-naming advice, see Shannon Combs-Bennett's guide <www.familytreemagazine.com/premium/5-genealogy-filing-systems>.

the PDF file, too. That way, if someone downloads the file, they'll still have all the details about the document. For example, I added pages with a title, introduction and name index to my grandmother Osa Olmsted's diary on FamilySearch <bit.ly/30qWJP7>. ●

Rick Crume is gradually digitizing his large collection of family photos and records.

Crunching Numbers

Keep track of the people in your family tree with these genealogical numbering systems, such as *Ahnentafel* and the Register System.

by DREW SMITH

In our modern digital world, keeping track of our ancestors is relatively easy. Using desktop genealogy software, we can quickly produce lists of ancestors or descendants, search for people with particular names, or display clickable pedigree charts that allow us to move from one person to another. We can even take two people from different parts of our family tree, and a tool will instantly tell us how they are related to each other.

But the pre-computer genealogical world was completely different. Producing large family trees in a visual format demanded tedious work, and figuring out exactly how ancestors might be related to the researcher required large hand-drawn charts and lots of reading. It was especially tricky when multiple ancestors had the same name. And studying the *descendants* of an ancestor was even more laborious, requiring tracking thousands of individuals.

This was the information-management issue studied by some of the best late-19th- and early-20th-century genealogists. As they began to generate large written family histories or publish their research in the new genealogy journals of the day, they realized they needed some sort of system to number their direct ancestors or the descendants of a famous ancestor. Numbering could help distinguish two different people with the exact same name, identify which generation they fit into, and even specify the birth order of children within a family.

Even today, with our genealogy software, we still find it helpful to use some of these numbering systems in order to produce lists and reports, especially when sharing with others. I wouldn't be surprised to find a few current genealogists *still* trying to design a better numbering system, or at least tinkering with existing systems in order to improve them.

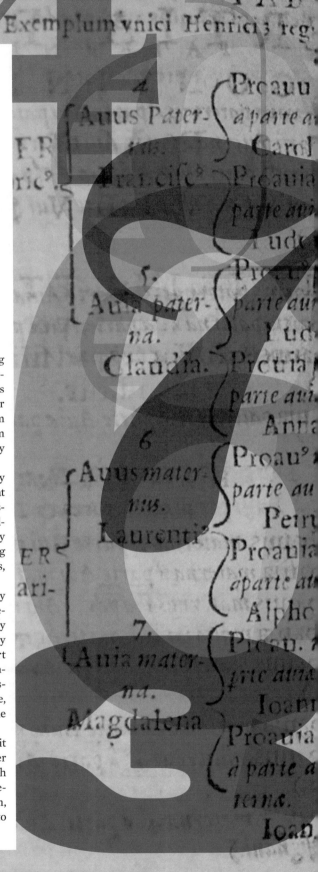

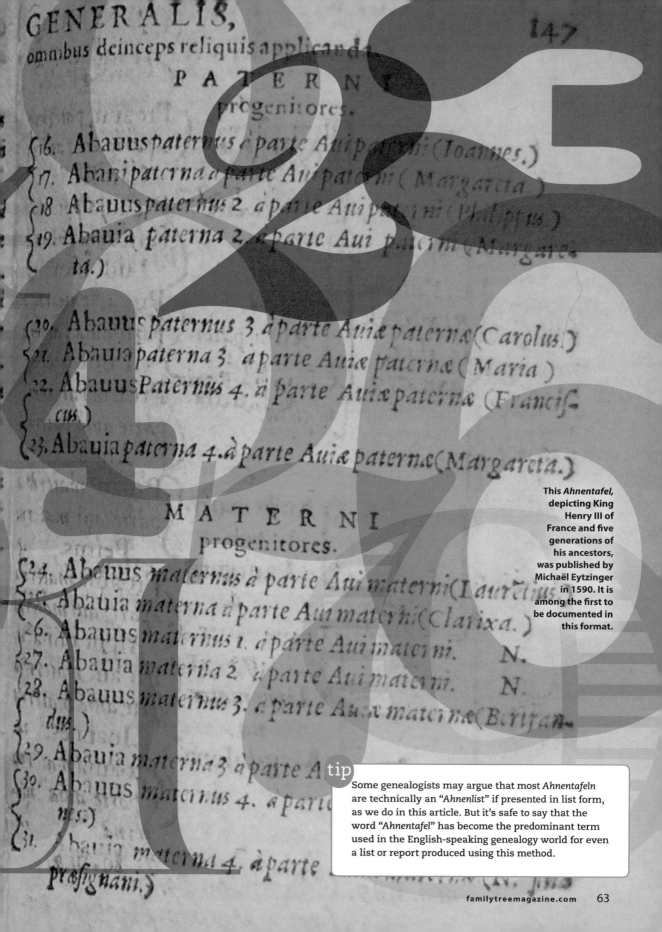

GENERALIS,

omnibus deinceps reliquis applicanda

PATERNI

progenitores.

6. Abauuspaternus à parte Aui paterni (Ioannes.)

17. Abani paterna à parte Aui paterni (Margareta.)

18. Abauuspaternus 2. à parte Aui paterni (Philippus.)

19. Abauia paterna 2. à parte Aui paterni (Margareta.)

20. Abauus paternus 3. à parte Auiæ paternæ (Carolus.)

21. Abauia paterna 3. à parte Auiæ paternæ (Maria)

22. Abauus Paternus 4. à parte Auiæ paternæ (Francisc̄us.)

23. Abauia paterna 4. à parte Auiæ paternæ (Margareta.)

MATERNI

progenitores.

24. Abauus maternus à parte Aui materni (Laurentius)

25. Abauia materna à parte Aui materni (Clarixa.)

26. Abauus maternus 1. à parte Aui materni. N.

27. Abauia materna 2. à parte Aui materni. N.

28. Abauus maternus 3. à parte Auiæ maternæ (Bertrandus.)

29. Abauia materna 3 à parte A

30. Abauus maternus 4. à parte

31. abauia materna 4. à parte

præsignani.)

This *Ahnentafel,* depicting King Henry III of France and five generations of his ancestors, was published by Michaël Eytzinger in 1590. It is among the first to be documented in this format.

tip

Some genealogists may argue that most *Ahnentafeln* are technically an "*Ahnenlist*" if presented in list form, as we do in this article. But it's safe to say that the word "*Ahnentafel*" has become the predominant term used in the English-speaking genealogy world for even a list or report produced using this method.

William I 1066 - 1087 / William II 1087 - 1100 / Henry I 1100 - 1135 / Stephen 1135 - 1154 / Henry II 1154 - 1189 / Richard I 1189 - 1199 / John 1199 - 1216 / Henry III 1216 - 1272 / Edward I 1272 - 1307 / Edward II 1307 - 1327

The Royal Family Tree

Throughout this article, we use the British royal family as it was in early 2021 to demonstrate each genealogical numbering system. If you need a refresher on how that family is structured, we've put together this partial family tree of Queen Elizabeth II and her grandson William, Duke of Cambridge. (Note: For space, we've omitted some members of the royal family, such as spouses who are ancestors to William. You can find a full, up-to-date family tree at <www.bbc.com/news/uk-23272491>.)

*In early 2021, Princess Eugenie gave birth to a son named August (not shown).

Whether you're one of those pioneering long-haulers or a beginner genealogist wanting to use an existing system, let's take a deep dive into the world of genealogical numbering systems. They can be divided into three types: ancestral, descendant, and combination.

Note: We'll demonstrate each system using the genealogy of a famous pedigree, the royal family of the United Kingdom (with Queen Elizabeth II or her son William, Duke of Cambridge, as the root person). For reference, you can see a more traditional family tree of Elizabeth II's direct-line descendants (including her grandson William) on the opposite page.

ANCESTRAL-NUMBERING SYSTEMS: THE *AHNENTAFEL* SYSTEM

Keeping track of direct ancestors in a numbering system is reasonably straightforward, so it should not be surprising that the earliest example of such a system can be found more than 400 years ago. Austrian historian Michaël Eytzinger published a genealogical work (*Thesaurus Principum Hac Aetate In Europa Viventium*) documenting royal European houses in 1590.

This Eytzinger Method, known in German as an *Ahnentafel* (in English, "ancestor table"), was picked up by two later genealogists: Jerónimo de Sosa and Stephan Kekulé von Stradonitz. Sosa, a Spanish Franciscan friar and genealogist, wrote about the method in 1676 in his work *Noticia de la Gran Casa de los Marqueses de Villafranca*. And von Stradonitz, a German lawyer and genealogist, popularized the Ahnentafel method in his 1898 work *Ahnentafel-Atlas: Ahnentafeln zu 32 Ahnen der Regenten Europas und ihrer Gemahlinnen*.

The *Ahnentafel* method is easy to describe. The root person (say, the genealogist) is assigned the number 1. From there, the system doubles a person's number to get the number for No. 1's father and adds one to *that* number to get the number for their mother. So the root person's father is 2 and their mother is 3. The pattern continues as you move back in generations: Their paternal grandfather is 4, their paternal grandmother is 5, their maternal grandfather is 6, and their maternal grandmother is 7. The system can be carried back as many generations as one has names, leaving out those numbers where the names are unknown.

Let's see how this works in practice for Prince William, Duke of Cambridge, back to his great-grandparents:

1. Prince William, Duke of Cambridge
2. Charles, Prince of Wales
3. Lady Diana Spencer
4. Prince Philip, Duke of Edinburgh
5. Elizabeth II of the United Kingdom
6. John Spencer, 8th Earl Spencer
7. The Honourable Frances Roche
8. Prince Andrew of Greece and Denmark
9. Princess Alice of Battenberg
10. George VI of the United Kingdom
11. Elizabeth Bowes-Lyon, The Queen Mother
12. Albert Spencer, 7th Earl Spencer
13. Lady Cynthia Hamilton
14. Maurice Roche, 4th Baron Fermoy
15. Ruth Sylvia Gill

In the *Ahnentafel* System, a person's number can instantly provide certain kinds of information. For instance, the parents are 2 through 3, the grandparents are 4 through 7, the great-grandparents are 8 through 15, and so forth. This allows us to figure out how many generations back an individual is by seeing which range the person's number falls into. From a mathematical perspective, patrilineal lines are simple powers of two: 2, 4, 8, 16, etc. Matrilineal lines are one less than powers of two: 3, 7, 15, 31, etc.

However, even a simple system like the *Ahnentafel* method can run into some snags. If we were to continue the numbers for Prince William's ancestors, we would eventually reach the royal couple Christian IX, King of Denmark, and Princess Louise of Hesse-Kassel. They are numbers 32 and 33, as they are the great-grandparents of number 4, Prince Philip. But they are also numbers 82 and 83, as they are the great-great-grandparents of Elizabeth II. In fact, Queen Victoria is both 79 and 81! (Elizabeth II and Prince Philip, both great-great-grandchildren of Queen Victoria, are third cousins.)

Welcome to pedigree collapse! In any culture that does not forbid the marriage of known relatives, you are likely going to witness this phenomenon. Sooner or later, as you trace your direct ancestors back through the generations, the same individual or couple will appear in different parts of your family tree.

This means that they would be given more than one *Ahnentafel* number to represent them.

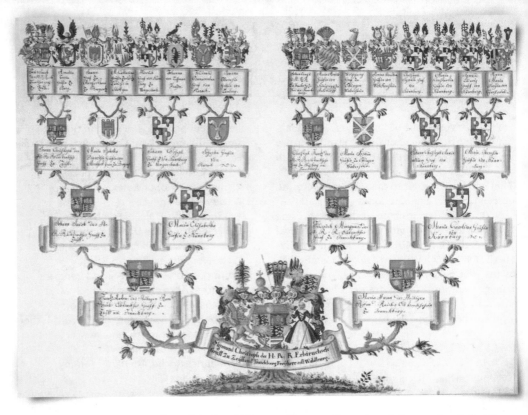

A 1776 *Ahnentafel* of Sigmund Christoph Graf von Waldburg-Zeil-Trauchburg, a German bishop

The usual solution (if you're doing it by hand) is to mark the higher number with an indication that it duplicates a lower number.

Another drawback: Should new genealogical research change the knowledge of which person is the parent of a known ancestor, this would mean re-assigning numbers for those individuals and their ancestors going backwards. But genealogy software makes this easy to do.

The last problem that might be an issue with the *Ahnentafel* system is if you want to assign numbers to both biological ancestors *and* adopted ancestors. A common solution is to add an *A* (for "adopted") or a *B* (for "biological" or "birth") to the number, to indicate the nature of the relationship. So far as I'm aware, current genealogical software does not provide this feature, although it would be a handy one.

Also, in the case of an adoption by a same-sex couple, the usual procedure of assigning the even number to the male parent and the odd number to the female parent would need to be modified, perhaps by instead assigning the even number to the older parent and the odd number to the younger parent.

DESCENDANT-NUMBERING SYSTEMS

Designing a numbering system for *descendants* is much less straightforward than designing one for ancestors. The root person (that is, the famous ancestor or other person of interest) is still generally assigned the number 1. But there are several choices to be made about how to number his or her descendants.

We'll discuss four systems in this section, but each of them has an obvious flaw: The discovery of a previously unknown child in a family (or an erroneous inclusion of a child) will mean that many numbers will have to be re-assigned. While genealogical software can easily do the re-numbering, this will still invalidate at least part of the numbering of any previously published or otherwise shared reports.

The Register System

One key question to ask as you decide which system to use: Do you assign numbers for only those descendants who had offspring, or for all descendants regardless? The two most popular descendant-numbering systems have made this choice differently.

The New England Historic Genealogical Society (NEHGS) <www.americanancestors.org>, founded in 1845, is the oldest genealogical society in the United States, and it's published its quarterly journal, *The New England Historical and Genealogical Register*, for nearly as long. By 1870, the *Register* adopted a numbering system that assigned Arabic numbers to only those descendants who themselves produced children. Numbers are assigned by family group, in age order.

In the *Ahnentafel* System, knowing a person's number can instantly provide us with certain kinds of information

Let's see how the Register System would work for the descendants of Queen Elizabeth II:

1. **Queen Elizabeth II**
2. **Charles, Prince of Wales**
3. **Anne, Princess Royal**
4. **Andrew, Duke of York**
5. **Edward, Earl of Wessex**
6. **William, Duke of Cambridge**
7. **Harry, Duke of Sussex**
8. **Peter Phillips**
9. **Zara Tindall**
10. **Princess Eugenie of York**

Note that numbers are assigned in family groups. So, for example, Charles' children William and Harry have numbers 6 and 7 despite being younger than their cousins Peter and Zara (numbers 8 and 9). Because Charles is the eldest of his siblings, his children have the first numbers of that generation.

The NGSQ System (or Modified Register System)

Likewise, the National Genealogical Society (NGS) <www.ngsgenealogy.org> was founded in 1903 and in 1912 began publishing its journal, the *National Genealogical Society Quarterly* (NGSQ). That publication, too, developed its own descendant-numbering system, distinct from that of the *NEHGS Register*.

Although there are a number of differences between the NGSQ System (also known as the Record System or Modified Register System) and the Register System, the primary difference is that *all* descendants in the NGSQ System, regardless of whether they have children, are assigned their own Arabic number.

But, like in the Register System, numbers are assigned by family group in birth order. Those who have children are marked with a + sign in reports to indicate descendants.

> Access to the *National Genealogy Society Quarterly* journal is a benefit of joining NGS. Learn about more about common membership perks at genealogy societies <www.familytreemagazine.com/general-genealogy/5-reasons-you-should-join-a-genealogy-society>.

Here is how the numbering would look for the descendants of Queen Elizabeth II:

1. **Queen Elizabeth II**
2. **Charles, Prince of Wales**
3. **Anne, Princess Royal**
4. **Andrew, Duke of York**
5. **Edward, Earl of Wessex**
6. **William, Duke of Cambridge**
7. **Harry, Duke of Sussex**
8. **Peter Phillips**
9. **Zara Tindall**
10. **Princess Beatrice of York**
11. **Princess Eugenie of York**
12. **Lady Louise Windsor**
13. **James, Viscount Severn**
14. **Prince George of Cambridge**
15. **Princess Charlotte of Cambridge**
16. **Prince Louis of Cambridge**
17. **Archie Harrison Mountbatten-Windsor**
18. **Savannah Phillips**
19. **Isla Phillips**
20. **Mia Grace Tindall**
21. **Lena Elizabeth Tindall**
22. **August Brooksbank**

Like in the Register System, the numbering by family group means that some descendants are listed before their same-generation cousins, even if they were born after them.

As you can see, these two systems produce sequential numbers for descendants. But the numbers, by themselves, do not provide other information such as which generation the person falls into or what birth order each person would have in the larger family. However, generation-numbering and birth-order numbering are part of the full stylings of both the Register and NGSQ Systems.

The Henry System

While the Register System and the NGSQ System are the most popular descendancy-numbering systems in use, two others are worth mentioning: the Henry System and the d'Aboville System. Though similar to one other, they each have unique benefits, and you'll find them as additional options in such desktop genealogy software as Family Tree Maker <www.mackiev.com/ftm> and RootsMagic <www.rootsmagic.com>.

The Henry System was designed by Reginald Buchanan Henry, and he used it in his 1935 work *Genealogies of the Families of the Presidents*. Like the others we've discussed, it assigns 1 to the root person. But then it adds a digit for each generation, and the value of that digit is the birth order in their family unit.

This is what it would look like for the descendants of Queen Elizabeth II:

1. Queen Elizabeth II
  11. Charles, Prince of Wales
    111. William, Duke of Cambridge
      1111. Prince George of Cambridge
      1112. Princess Charlotte of Cambridge
      1113. Prince Louis of Cambridge
    112. Harry, Duke of Sussex
      1121. Archie Mountbatten-Windsor
  12. Anne, Princess Royal
    121. Peter Phillips
      1211. Savannah Phillips
      1212. Isla Phillips
    (and so on)

This system can also accommodate the root person's siblings. In the above arrangement, Elizabeth II's younger sister, Princess Margaret, would be number 2, and Margaret's children David and Sarah would be 21 and 22 respectively.

It might occur to you that the Henry System would run into some problems, including in the case of families with more than nine children. But the system has an answer: The 10th child is marked with an *X*, while additional children are marked *A*, *B*, *C*, and so forth. In some variations (such as the Modified Henry System), the 10th and later children have their birth orders put into parentheses.

The d'Aboville System

Although the d'Aboville System is attributed to Count Jacques d'Aboville in 1940, one can find an example of essentially the same system being used as early as 1915 by the Huntington Family Association in its publications. The primary difference between the Henry and d'Aboville Systems is that the generation digits are separated by periods, so that 11 in the Henry System is 1.1 in the d'Aboville System. This solves the problem of birth order numbers larger than nine.

So the descendants of Queen Elizabeth II would be numbered:

Above: St. Edward's Crown, used to crown the British monarch; above right: then-Princess Elizabeth and Prince Philip (front, center) amid the royal family on their wedding day, 1947

1. Queen Elizabeth II
  1.1. Charles, Prince of Wales
    1.1.1. William, Duke of Cambridge
      1.1.1.1. Prince George of Cambridge
      1.1.1.2. Princess Charlotte of Cambridge
      1.1.1.3. Prince Louis of Cambridge
    1.1.2. Harry, Duke of Sussex
      1.1.2.1. Archie Mountbatten-Windsor
  1.2. Anne, Princess Royal
    1.2.1. Peter Phillips
      1.2.1.1. Savannah Phillips
      1.2.1.2. Isla Phillips
    (and so on)

OTHER SYSTEMS AND COMMON ERRORS

Is it possible to create a system that will assign a number to *all* of your direct ancestors, as well as all of their descendants? Yes, such as by combining the *Ahnentafel* system with one of the descendancy systems.

For instance, you could combine *Ahnentafel* numbering for ancestors with d'Aboville numbering for descendants. If the root person were Prince William (he would be assigned number

1), his father, Charles, would be 2. Then Prince Harry (William's brother) could be 2.2 or 3.2, as the second child of No. 2 Charles and No. 3 Diana. (This solution is also a good workaround to document half-siblings.)

But what about assigning numbers to the spouses of our non-ancestor relatives? Numbering systems don't generally include these individuals. Noted genealogist William Dollarhide has suggested adding an asterisk to the relative's number to designate the spouse, and to add *1, *2, etc. in the case of multiple spouses. In other cases, you might simply add an S to a person's number to generate a figure for the spouse.

As you might imagine, there are a few other numbering systems in the genealogical world. All systems are going to have their pluses and minuses, so I'm doubtful that a perfect system will ever be designed. Fortunately, current genealogy software automatically handles all the numbering for us, and we can switch between the popular systems as often as we like as we produce reports.

If you'd like to know a bit more about the details of these systems and how to handle unique situations, you'll enjoy *Numbering Your Genealogy: Basic Systems, Complex Families, and International Kin* by Joan Ferris Curran, Madilyn Coen Crane, and John H. Wray (National Genealogical Society), published in 2008.

Drew Smith is the genealogy librarian at the University of South Florida Libraries in Tampa, host of the Genealogy Connection podcast, and cohost of The Genealogy Guys Podcast. His book, *Organize Your Genealogy: Strategies and Solutions for Every Researcher* (Family Tree Books), was published in 2016. Drew now writes regularly for the *Association of Professional Genealogists Quarterly* on the topic of productivity.

> Find more tips for organizing your genealogy on our landing page, which includes links to articles on reducing paper clutter, genealogy filing systems, organization tech tools and more <www.familytreemagazine.com/organize-genealogy>.

The End of the Paper Trail

Cutting paper clutter will make you better organized and sharpen your genealogy focus. Get started with these 12 less-paper strategies.

BY DENISE MAY LEVENICK

✢ **DOING GENEALOGY SOMETIMES** feels more like pushing paper than pursuing ancestors. Binders, folders, journals, books, printouts and notes can create a roadblock more daunting than your most challenging brick wall.

Still, many genealogists cringe at the word *paperless*. They love the sound of freshly printed documents slipping out of the printer tray. They like marking up hard copies with highlighters and cross-referencing current research with old notes. Paper *lasts*, they say: Printed notes and records don't disappear with the crash of a hard drive. You don't need a special device to read a 100-year-old letter on paper—unlike a digital document, which requires a computer and compatible software.

That's true, of course. But managing a mountain of paper costs you money, space and time. Printers, ink, paper and filing supplies get expensive. Space to keep it all is at a premium in many homes. Paper overflowing on your desk, in drawers and on shelves dilutes your focus, and organizing it takes away from research time.

So what if you claim territory in the middle ground, where you thoughtfully select which papers you really need, dispose of the rest and develop habits that keep more paper from entering your home? Not *paperless*, but *less paper*. We'll show you 12 ways to navigate a path to less genealogy paper and more genealogy productivity.

1 Know where you're going.

The first step in planning a journey is knowing where you're going—having a target destination that serves as your goal. So set a goal to reduce your paper load. Focusing on your destination will make it easier to eliminate the unnecessary paper in your genealogy life. As a result, your research will be more enjoyable and the paper documents that are most important to manage and preserve will receive the attention they deserve.

2 Sort out original documents.

Family historians work with two different kinds of paper: original documents and photos on one hand, and working copies on the other. Each type calls for different handling and digitizing methods, so you'll want to separate them as you go through your piles of paper.

Heirloom originals include old documents (such as baptismal, birth and marriage certificates), old books (family Bibles and journals), original photographs, letters, newspaper clippings, funeral cards and other paper ephemera that holds genealogical information. You also might include photocopies of records made while doing on-site research, letterhead from Grandpa's business and other one-of-a-kind paper documents. If it would be a financial or logistical burden to replace the item, consider it an original. These are the paper files you want to organize and preserve as your research archive.

For the purposes of reducing paper, most record images that you've viewed on websites such as Ancestry.com <ancestry.com>, FamilySearch <www.familysearch.org> and MyHeritage <www.myheritage.com>, then downloaded to your computer and printed out, aren't original documents. Your relatives' census, land, probate, estate and other public records may have been difficult to locate online, but original copies are still available on those same websites. File the digital copy, enter extracted information in your tree, and keep a record of the citation (which you can use if you ever need to find the document online again). Then recycle the printouts of the record.

3 Gather your working documents.

Your everyday handwritten and computerized research notes belong with your working documents. It's not necessary to print out a new family group sheet every time you add information to your genealogy software. If you regularly back up your computer (see more on this in step 10), that information is safe in its "born digital" format, so don't waste the paper.

Other working documents include magazines and newsletters, receipts, research logs and plans, printed results from library catalog searches, pedigree charts and other reports,

> If it would be a financial or logistical burden to replace the item, consider it an original.

email messages, downloaded books and documents from genealogy websites, and anything created digitally. Organize these on your hard drive and print them only as needed (such as charts to take to a family reunion or catalog results to take to the library). You'll digitize hard-copy heirloom and working documents in the next couple of steps.

4 Scan heirloom documents.

Heirloom originals and working documents call for different methods of digitization. You'd probably hand-wash a pricey new car with special towels and cleaners instead of a hose-end scrub brush, at least for a while. Your heirloom documents need that "white glove" treatment, too. In fact, it's a good idea to wear white cotton gloves, or keep your hands scrupulously clean, when handling old photos and negatives.

Never digitize your heirloom originals with a standard sheet-fed office scanner. Old, brittle or damaged paper can easily become jammed or even shredded in the roller mechanism of such equipment. Play it safe by digitizing your priceless documents on a flatbed scanner, saving files in a TIFF or JPG format (find scanning tips at <familytreemagazine.com/article/scanning-family-photos>). For books, scan one page at a time by placing half the book on the scanner glass and letting the other side hang off the edge.

Another "scanning" option, especially for books and large documents, is to photograph them with your digital camera using a tripod for sharp, shake-free images. I like the Joby Gorillapod <www.joby.com>, which is flexible so you can stand it up or wrap it around a railing or chair back. Place the document flat on a table or the floor and position the camera directly over it. Using a remote shutter release will prevent the "shutter shake" that happens as you press the shutter.

If you travel frequently, it's smart to digitize on the go rather than accumulating bits of paper to scan and organize when you return to your home office. If you use your camera to digitize while on a research trip, immediately upload the images to cloud storage (see step 11) so you have a backup.

Smartphone apps such as CamScanner and
Turboscan help you turn your phone into a scanner
for preserving photos and documents.

5 Winnow and digitize working documents.

Chances are, working documents make up the bulk of your paper mountain. These working papers require efficient digitizing to help you conquer that mountain in good time. But first, if you no longer need the paper, don't scan it. Notes about a research problem you've since resolved? Toss it. Travel itinerary for last year's genealogy conference? Get rid of it. Brochures you picked up that you'll never use? Put them in the recycling.

You probably already own some kind of scanner or digitizing device. Many home offices include an all-in-one printer-copier-scanner that can handle most office chores. These efficient models save space in small offices, and offer basic printing, scanning and copying functions best for digitizing letter- or legal-size papers or photos. They often include a sheet-fed mechanism that can speed up larger scanning jobs, but scan time per page is usually slower than with a dedicated sheet-fed scanner. You also might find that the software included with an all-in-one scanner offers fewer options (such as for resolution or document type) than a dedicated flatbed or sheet-fed scanner. If you regularly scan a lot of paper or you need to scan film or slides, consider getting a specialized scanner. In that case, you'll save considerable time by using a high-speed duplex sheet-fed scanner such as the Fujitsu ScanSnap **<fujitsuscannerstore.com/scanners/scansnap>** or

Neat Document Scanner **<neat.com>**. These devices offe several advantages:

- Duplex scanning digitizes both sides of the paper at th same time, effectively cutting your scan time in half.
- Batch processing allows you to set a file name for a entire batch of items further identified by a unique number
- Automatic sheet feed mechanism dispatches pages on at a time through the scanner
- Optical Character Recognition (OCR) software ma offer the ability to turn printed text into searchable text
- Multiple file format options allow you to scan directly t PDF, JPG, TIFF or other format.

Your smartphone is another option for mobile warriors, o anyone away from home. Adding an inexpensive app such a CamScanner **<camscanner.com>**, Genius Scan **<thegrizzlylabs.com** or Turbo Scan **<turboscanapp.com>** turns your device into a scan ner. Scanning apps offer several advantages over the standar camera app included with your smartphone, especially the abi ity to crop as you scan. Most apps allow you to rename the fi and add numbering, dates or other information. Scan your trave receipts and toss the originals. These digital versions are no accepted by virtually all accountants for tax-reporting purpose

Adjust your workflow.

Begin your move toward less paper clutter by creating only digital documents, keeping them in digital format until you need a printed copy. This may mean breaking old habits: If you usually find a record online, download it, and then automatically go for the Print button, you'll have to stop yourself. Instead, download the record, name it (see step 7) and file it on your hard drive (step 8).

When you find text you want to save on a website, you have a few options besides printing it out. You could:

- use a note-taking program such as Evernote to "clip" the portion of the website you want to save and store the clipping with a link to the source site in an Evernote note. You'll undoubtedly find Evernote useful in many ways, including keeping research notes you can access using your computer, tablet or mobile phone. Learn how to manage your genealogy research with Evernote in *How to Use Evernote for Genealogy* Family Tree Books) .

- take a screenshot or copy the part of the website you want and paste it into a Word document to save.

- bookmark the site to revisit later, although this has some drawbacks—the site could go offline or change URLs, or you might forget why you bookmarked the site.

Don't print email messages. Instead, extract any information you want to add as notes in your genealogy software or digitized research log, then file the message in a Correspondence folder in your in-box. If you haven't already done so, make your email account easy to access from your smartphone or tablet by downloading the service's mobile app.

Eliminate more clutter by converting paper publications you receive to digital editions. Get digitized books instead of the print version, request your conference syllabus as a PDF or on disc, opt for the digital version of your society's newsletter, and order digital subscriptions to your favorite magazines (including *Family Tree Magazine*). Save these documents in your digital filing system for quick access.

Consistently name digital files.

Use a consistent file-naming scheme for genealogy records to help you easily locate the digital version on your computer, and know what's in a file before you open it. Get in the habit of renaming the file as soon as you download it. I use a four-part scheme that includes last name, first name, date, location, and event in that order, for example, *smith-john_1930_texas-dallas_census*.

Some researchers prefer to begin the filename with a date; others prefer the surname. Think about the alphabetical sorting ability of your computer when deciding how to name your files. Files beginning with a year will sort chronologically, as shown below; files beginning with a surname will group by name. Whatever scheme you choose, make a cheat sheet to hang next to your computer as a reminder.

Use a simple folder structure.

As you collect more digital files, you'll need a way to organize them so you can find them again. Many genealogists use a simple folder arrangement with all genealogy-related files inside one big folder labeled Genealogy. This folder could contain subfolders for genealogical societies, genetic genealogy, places you're searching, and surnames you're researching. Inside the Surnames folder, you could set up a folder for each surname you're tracing. Those folders would hold digitized records for people with that surname. You could go further to create folders for each nuclear family, for example, SMITH Alex and Rebecca. In this case, place

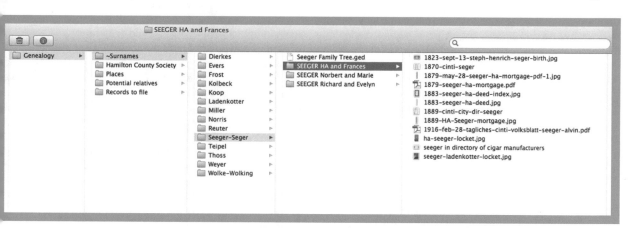

Storing digital files inside a Genealogy folder on your computer hard drive makes it easier to set up automatic file backup of your research materials. One way to structure your files is in folders for surnames (a tilde, or ~, before the file name causes it to sort to the top of the folder list), places and other topics important to your search. Then you can file record images by nuclear family. A Potential Relatives folder is a handy place for records of folks who are probably relatives, but you're not yet sure how.

Rebecca's records in her parents' folder until she marries, then put them in her folder with her husband.

In the Places folder, you could keep maps of towns where your ancestors lived, background information, and digitized county histories that apply to multiple families. Folders for genealogy societies could hold calendars, digitized newsletters and notes from meetings.

Being consistent with your folder structure will help you easily find the files you need and back up your work.

9 Take advantage of software.

Many genealogists use their genealogy database software as tool to manage digital files. Genealogy programs are available as standalone desktop software (such as Family Tree Maker <www.mackiev.com/ftm>, Legacy Family Tree <www.legacyfamilytree.com>, RootsMagic <www.rootsmagic.com> or Family Tree Builder <www.familytreebuilder.com>) or cloud-based family tree applications (such as MyHeritage or Ancestry.com). Many family tree sites combine these options with online trees that sync with desktop software, so you have copies in both places and can edit either one. MyHeritage trees, for example, sync with Family Tree Builder software, and Family Tree Maker software syncs with trees on Ancestry.com (RootsMagic soon will sync with Ancestry trees as well).

Whether desktop or online, genealogy programs let you create a family tree by adding people manually or uploading a GEDCOM file (the basic file format for genealogy software). Many programs also let you attach photos and digitized records, along with source information, to ancestor profiles, helping you connect your sources to family members.

Even when you attach record images to individuals in your software or online tree, keep a master copy of these research images filed on your hard drive, where you can regularly back them up. Don't assume your software or a genealogy website will always be there. Like any other business, genealogy companies can cease operation or change policies and accessibility at any time. Family Tree Maker users panicked at the end of 2015, when Ancestry.com announced it would stop producing the software and end syncing with online trees. Although users got a reprieve when Software MacKiev <www.mackiev.com> acquired the program and promised to

TIP: If you have research papers relevant to someone else's family—but not yours—consider donating them to your local genealogical or historical society library. Call first to ask about donation policies, and look for a facility related to your family history.

PAPER SHORTCUTS

These simple strategies will help you keep your finger off the Print button and cut your genealogy paper clutter:

■ **SAVE TO PDF:** Resist the temptation to print out newly updated files. Instead, use the Save to PDF or Print to PDF option, available in Microsoft Word and many other software programs. As a bonus, you can find full-text searchable PDF documents faster on your computer than by digging through file folders in a drawer.

■ **SUBSCRIBE TO DIGITAL:** As your magazine subscriptions and genealogical society memberships come up for renewal, select the option to receive publications digitally if available. You might save money, you'll have less paper to manage and you can access your subscriptions on your tablet.

■ **CONVERT TO DIGITAL:** Are your shelves and drawers weighed down with journals, conference syllabi and notebooks? One you've culled your collection, remove the bindings from the "keepers" and run the pages through a sheet-fed scanner to create your own PDF reference library. Respect authors' copyright by recycling the originals and limiting the digital versions to your own use.

continue it, the situation serves as a reminder to keep a personal copy of your own content.

10 Back up your digitized files.

If you've recently started trying to go paperless, you may have a nagging fear that a flood or electrical surge will fry your hard drive and *pouf!*—your digitized files will disappear. This could happen, which is why you should remember LOCKSS: Lots of Copies Keeps Stuff Safe. A single copy of your files isn't a backup, especially if it's on the same hard drive as the original data. A true backup includes three or more copies, each located on a different kind of storage media, such as computer hard drive, external hard drive, DVD (provided you have a DVD drive), or online in cloud storage (see step 11).

If you've already organized your computer files with genealogy information in one big Genealogy folder, it's a simple matter to back up that folder to multiple locations for safekeeping or mobile access. Do this at least monthly or after a research session. You'll also want a full computer backup to protect photos, videos and other information stored on your hard drive.

11 Brave the cloud.

Cloud storage can seem like stormy weather: uncertain and a bit scary. We all use "the cloud" every time we access the internet; cloud storage means merely that you're storing data on remote servers instead of on your home computer. Each time you access your bank or utility statements online, you're using the cloud storage offered by your bank or phone company.

Cloud storage services such as Backblaze **<backblaze.com>** and Google Drive **<google.com/drive>** let you store almost any kind of digital file on a remote server, where it's safe from disasters that could befall your computer. You'll also be able to access stored documents from other devices, decreasing the need to carry around flash drives and printed copies.

Ideally, you want a cloud storage service that automatically backs up your computer whenever you're online, so you won't even have to think about it.

MORE ONLINE

Web Content

■ Organize genealogy email **<familytreemagazine.com/article/organize-your-genealogy-email>**

■ How to organize your hard drive **<familytreemagazine.com/article/feb-2012-make-over-hard-drive>**

■ Eight tips to organize your research **<familytreemagazine.com/article/win-the-paper-chase>**

■ Your ideal genealogy workspace **<familytreemagazine.com/organization/makeover-genealogy-workspace>**

■ How to back up your research **<familytreemagazine.com/article/genealogy-backup-basics>**

■ Using a document scanner for genealogy **<familytreemagazine.com/article/document-scanners-for-genealogy>**

12 Pack your toolbox.

Reducing your genealogy paper clutter isn't just getting rid of unnecessary papers. It's also avoiding the addition of more paper to your home. Stocking your computer and mobile devices with the following types of apps and tools will help you digitize your papers and keep you from having to hit the Print button. Look for these tools in your device's app store or on the websites listed:

■ the app for your genealogy software so you can access your tree while on research trips

■ an app, such as Camscanner, that turns smartphone photos into PDFs

■ a note-taking app such as Evernote or Zotero **<www.zotero.org>**, where you can keep a research log (tag the notes "To Do"), source citations, etc.

■ Google Drive or Microsoft OneDrive to keep data in spreadsheets (another way to maintain a research log or source citations database) and store documents you want to access from anywhere

■ Scrivener **<www.literatureandlatte.com/scrivener.php>**, software (with a companion mobile app for iOS) that helps you write your family history while viewing digitized resources side-by-side

■ genealogy conference apps, when available, to get course schedules and exhibit hall information on your phone (search for the name of the conference in your device's app store)

■ a calendar app, such as Google's (search your device's app store), where you can store all the details about events on your schedule

■ a travel app such as TripIt **<www.tripit.com>**, which organizes your itineraries for easy access on your phone

■ Google Maps or another app so you won't have to print driving directions

■ an app to organize all your e-books, such as Calibre **<calibre-ebook.com>**

Navigating through your paper clutter doesn't have to be an impossible digital dream. Set aside some time each week to devote to your paperless efforts, and commit to reducing the amount of paper you bring into your home. With planning and the proper tools, you can reduce your paper load to gain more time and better focus for your genealogy research. ■

....

DENISE LEVENICK is the Family Curator **<thefamilycurator.com>** and author of *How To Archive Family Photos* and *How To Archive Family Keepsakes*, both from Family Tree Books.

KEEP OR TOSS?

Declutter your genealogy life with these three steps for determining what to keep and what to trash.

by LISA A. ALZO

Are you drowning in a sea

of papers, documents, old photographs, and other research materials? That's what genealogy is made of, but all that stuff can clutter your home and overwhelm you. There's only so much space, and having too many genealogical items makes it hard to access what you *really* need and pass research on to future generations.

What can you do with it all? There are really only two possibilities: toss it out, or keep it. Some objects are obvious "keeps" or trash. But what about the things in between? How can you determine what's worth saving?

If you feel more like a family history hoarder than historian, come on down and become a contestant on the genealogists' favorite game show, *Keep or Toss?* This three-step guide will help you win today's fabulous prize: a lean, well-curated family history collection.

Sorting List

As you work through your research materials, don't forget to parse through the following items:

- photos (both loose and in boxes) and photo albums
- unfiled papers
- digital files or emails you've printed
- family mementos
- passports or other identification documents
- vital certificates
- clothing, jewelry, medals, etc.
- china and glassware
- furniture
- newspaper clippings
- military paperwork and memorabilia
- memorial/funeral cards and books
- bridal books
- baby books
- yearbooks
- family newsletters
- receipts or utility bills
- old scrapbooks/autograph books
- postcards
- genealogy or history books
- county histories

STEP 1 SORT AND SEPARATE

No matter what the task is, your first step is always the same: Decide what you want to accomplish. Tackling a pare-down project is no different, but can feel overwhelming—particularly if you've been researching for years and are just now getting started.

You might remember that old saying: "How do you eat an elephant? One bite at a time." Apply this principle while going through your materials. Choose a box, container or photo album. (See the sidebar at left for a list of things to consider.) Remove everything and identify what each item is, then try to sort.

Create three sections on your table, desk, floor, or wherever you do your sorting: one for "Keep," one for "Donate," and one for "Toss." You may feel the need for a fourth area, "Undecided"; if you opt for that section, reserve it only for items you're *truly* uncertain about, and come back to them before the end of your session.

STEP 2 EVALUATE

The sad truth is that we can't keep everything. We've all heard tales of family treasures being sold off to flea markets or auctioned on eBay <www.ebay.com>. I've even heard of someone who rented a couple dumpsters and trashed his mother's belongings just a few days after her death.

Many people simply don't want more *stuff*, particularly younger generations who might not know the importance of antiques and heirlooms. Though it can be hard for genealogists to let go of anything that connects us to the past, we have to draw the line between packrat and curator.

And wouldn't it be better to personally decide the fate of your items, rather than having a (possibly uncaring) family member or estate-clearance company do it for you? There's a lot to be said for attending to as many of our own belongings as we can, before the inevitable happens. It's even the basis of a whole organization method: "Swedish death cleaning" <www.thespruce.com/swedish-death-cleaning-4801461>.

With that in mind, you'll need a framework for evaluating which of your items are worth keeping. First consider how much space you can comfortably allot for genealogy research and items. Then comes the hard part—determining what items are worth keeping and what aren't.

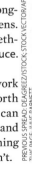

KEEP OR TOSS CHECKLIST

The Family Curator Denise May Levenick created a list of her recommendations about what to keep or toss in the July/August 2012 issue of *Family Tree Magazine*. Your list might differ based on the needs of your research, but Denise's suggestions can be a useful starting point. Download a digital version of the checklist at <www.familytreemagazine.com/freebie/family-history-stuff-keep-or-toss-checklist>.

KEEP

- vital records
- graduation, baby, marriage invitations and announcements
- educational records—school report cards, school photos
- military records—discharge papers, letters, awards
- Christmas cards and envelopes
- Christmas card lists
- recipes, especially handwritten favorites
- address books
- bank passbooks
- income tax returns
- journals, diaries, ledgers
- scrapbooks, autograph and photo albums
- correspondence
- employment records—pay stubs, contracts, résumés (keep enough to verify employment and salary)
- telephone books
- city and club directories and rosters
- genealogy and family history charts, narratives, family trees

SKIM, THEN TOSS

- church and club newsletters (skim first for family news and consider saving a representative copy)
- cancelled checks, check registers (skim first for purchases of family heirlooms or details on relatives' cost of living)
- news clippings (skim for news of family or friends)
- travel itineraries and brochures (skim for information on trips or places where relatives might live)
- old calendars (skim for anniversaries and dates of birth)
- receipts (skim for purchases of heirlooms and other important items such as automobiles)
- medical bills and records (extract genealogical information before throwing away)

TOSS

- random newspaper and magazine clippings
- bank statements
- old insurance policies (check first whether they're still in effect)
- travel brochures

Digital Decluttering

Besides paper and other physical possessions, your decluttering should include the many documents, photographs and other data you have on digital devices. Though digital decluttering probably won't save you much space in your home, it might very well bring you peace of mind. New Atlas <www.newatlas.com/computers/digital-hoarding-four-types-collectors-psychology> and the BBC <www.bbc.com/future/article/20190104-are-you-a-digital-hoarder> have both covered "digital hoarding" and how to overcome it.

Here are just some items to apply your "keep or toss?" criteria to:
- GEDCOMs and/or family tree files from genealogy software
- saved e-mails and social media posts
- digital images of records downloaded from genealogy websites
- scanned family photos and documents
- digital books and publications: ebooks, PDFs, etc.
- interview recordings (either audio or video)
- educational materials: downloaded webinars, podcasts, syllabi, and presentation handouts
- raw DNA test results
- website bookmarks

Back up important information you plan to keep to the cloud or an external hard drive, then delete the rest. If you're getting rid of a device, make sure to follow instructions so any personal data is *really* deleted and not residing in a cache that can be recovered.

One popular strategy has its roots in Japanese Shintoism. In 2011, organization consultant Marie Kondo published a book outlining her "KonMari" method. Translated into English as *The Life-Changing Magic of Tidying Up* (Ten Speed Press), the book suggests considering whether items "spark joy" when held. Those that do can stay, and those that don't should be thrown away. Owning only items that bring us joy, the KonMari method states, can bring clarity and peace of mind. The popularity of Kondo's method led to two popular reality TV series on Netflix.

While many embraced the KonMari method, others felt it was too extreme or placed too much emphasis on the idea of "joy." Regardless of what you think of Kondo's criteria, the method does highlight the importance of an organizational mindset.

For family historians, your sorting criteria should include assessments of an item's value and its ability to be passed on. Here are five important questions you might use to evaluate each item in your collection:

1. Is this item **irreplaceable** (i.e., one-of-a-kind)?
2. Is a **digital version** available? Would it be just as useful?
3. Who will **inherit** the information or item when I die? Will it be easy to store, and have others shown any interest in it?
4. What **practical value** is associated with the item? Is it worth a lot of money, or does it provide some intangible research benefit to you or descendants (for example, proving an ancestral line)?
5. What **sentimental value** is associated with the item? Does it represent a meaningful memory or person?

There aren't simple answers to these questions, and you'll need to consider each item in context. For example, some original documents can easily be digitized but don't have the same value when viewed as a scan: birth, marriage or death certificates; family Bibles; prayer books; photos; and so on. By comparison, my grandmother's electric bills (though original documents) wouldn't hold the same value for me as her original passport.

Other items may provide interesting information about your ancestor's time period, but not be worth saving in and of themselves. Receipts and pay stubs have some social history value, but you don't need to keep all of them. Select a few representative examples to scan, and discard the rest. Old family newsletters, too, are probably best scanned and saved as PDFs, then discarded.

Let's look at another example. Old newspapers or magazines take up a lot of space and decay quickly. (In fact, they can damage other materials as they do so!) And, because they were mass-produced, they're probably already available in digital formats. The Library of Congress <www.loc.gov/newspapers>, Newspapers.com <www.newspapers.com>, and GenealogyBank <www.genealogybank.com> are just a few websites that hold historical newspapers, and sites like Google Books <books.google.com> and the Internet Archive <www.archive.org> have digital copies of magazines and books. As a result, they probably aren't worth keeping unless they specifically mention someone in your family.

You might also think about what medium an item is in. Say you have 8mm film or Betamax video tapes, but no way of viewing them. Send the originals off to a digitization service so you can still access those family memories.

STEP 3 DONATE AND CURATE

For those items you choose to discard, do so safely and securely to protect any personal information. Consider using a shredding service, or (in special circumstances) burning items under controlled and legally permitted conditions. Be respectful of items such as worn-out flags <www.defense.gov/News/Feature-Stories/story/article/2206946/how-to-properly-dispose-of-worn-out-us-flags> and fragile items like glass.

Of course, not all items that you label "toss" *have* to go into a garbage can or recycling bin. Old jewelry can be parlayed into new creations, or clothes reconstituted into quilts or stuffed animals for younger generations. Or perhaps a family member is interested in taking certain items off your hands.

You can also make alternate arrangements for your items. Local charities will take furniture, clothing, books, and other useful items that are in good condition.

If you're getting rid of a sizeable, curated portion of your research, you could try bequeathing it to a local library, genealogical or historical society, or an ethnic organization. Start locally,

Want to cut down on the paper in your collection? Follow these 12 steps <www.familytreemagazine.com/organization/end-the-genealogy-paper-trail>.

Photo-Scanning Tips

You'll likely deem family photos worth keeping, but managing them (particularly if you have a lot) can be overwhelming. One solution is to create digital copies of all your photos, saving them from physical dangers like fire and flood.

As you plan to do so, try implementing the S.M.A.R.T. rule of goal-setting. This invites you to create goals that meet certain criteria—Specific, Measurable, Attainable/Actionable, Relevant/Realistic, and Time-bound—and will help you be more productive.

Here's how a goal of "I will scan all my family photos" might evolve via each of the S.M.A.R.T. criteria:

- *Specific*: I will scan all my family photos **using my V600 Epson scanner**.
- *Measurable*: I will scan **100** family photos using my V600 Epson scanner.
- *Attainable (Actionable)*: I will scan 100 family photos using my V600 Epson scanner **in four week-long sessions**.
- *Relevant (Realistic)*: I will scan 100 family photos using my V600 Epson scanner in four week-long sessions **of five photos per day**.
- *Time-bound*: I will scan 100 family photos using my V600 Epson scanner in four week-long sessions of five photos per day. **All photos will be scanned by January 1**.

and be sure to understand the organization's policies and guidelines. (Contact the curator directly, if necessary.)

On a wider level, the Genealogy Center of the Allen County Public Library <acpl.lib.in.us/donations> and the Family History Library <www.familysearch.org/en/wiki/Family_History_Library_Donations> each collect some genealogy papers, books, and other data, as do regional museums or archives. A quick online search will turn up organizations in your area (or in your ancestor's hometown) that could be the perfect new home for your family treasures. Consult Melissa Barker's "A Genealogist in the Archives" blog <agenealogistinthearchives.blogspot.com> for suggestions and tips.

One example is the Senator John Heinz History Center in Pittsburgh, which collects materials that document the lives of Western Pennsylvanians and the history of the region <www.heinzhistorycenter.org/collections/frequently-asked-questions>.

For heritage-specific items such as your great-grandpa's Russian military uniform, consider an ethnic genealogical society or museum. One such organization, The American Historical Society of Germans from Russia in Lincoln, Neb., presents rotating displays of donated items that German settlers brought with them from Russia. Their artifact and donation guidelines can be found at <www.ahsgr.org/library/donations>.

And what about items you're keeping? Store them using an archival-safe strategy. Use acid-free or buffered materials to prevent decay, and

keep items in a dark place with stable temperature and humidity.

Stock up on archival supplies, too, such as:
- white cotton or nitrile gloves to prevent leaving fingerprints while holding photos or negatives
- white butcher paper (available in rolls) to cover a sorting area
- archival-safe plastic clips to replace pins, staples and metal clips
- 3×5-index cards and markers to create labels (as opposed to using sticky labels, laminating, or writing directly on the items)

See <www.familytreemagazine.com/preservation/heirlooms/family-heirlooms> for more.

How you choose to organize the materials you intend to keep will depend on two primary factors: how you want to use the connection, and what available space you have.

Denise May Levenick, "The Family Curator," suggests working through materials carefully, considering each item in the collection before committing to an overall organization scheme. For example, do you need all or some of the items as part of an ongoing research project? If

Tap into 20-plus years of expert organization advice at <www.familytreemagazine.com/organize-genealogy>.

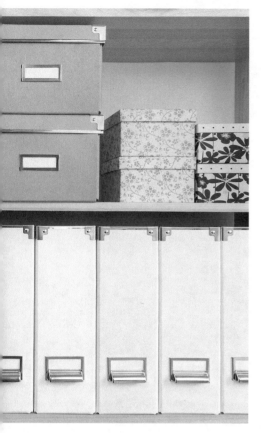

so, you'll want to keep the relevant items handy, and grouped together for easy access.

For my own keepsakes, I have a designated multi-tier shelf in a closet that is cool and dry. I organize materials by family line: a shelf for my Alzo line, a shelf for my Figlar line, and so on. I sub-divide by item type (photographs, documents, heirlooms, etc.) and store everything in an appropriate archival-safe box or container. All items are clearly labeled with the family name, the date and a brief description.

• • •

For genealogists, connections to the past are essential to learning about our ancestors. But we must also balance this and the need to preserve and share our research with future generations with less hassle and more joy. ●

Lisa A. Alzo is the author of *The Family Tree Polish, Czech and Slovak Genealogy Guide* (Family Tree Books). An avid genealogist for more than 30 years, she enjoys helping others discover their roots as an instructor for Family Tree University.

Toolkit: Downsizing Research

WEBSITES

40 Bags in 40 Days Decluttering Challenge <www.whitehouseblackshutters.com/40-bags-in-40-days-2014>

The Family Curator <www.thefamilycurator.com>

The Organized Genealogist Facebook Group <www.facebook.com/groups/organizedgenealogist>

The Photo Detective <www.maureentaylor.com>

ARCHIVAL PRODUCTS

Brodart <www.shopbrodart.com>

Gaylord Archival <www.gaylord.com>

Hollinger Metal Edge <www.hollingermetaledge.com>

BOOKS

Downsizing with Family History in Mind by Devon Noel Lee and Andrew Lee (FHF Group LLC)

The Gentle Art of Swedish Death Cleaning: How to Free Yourself and Your Family from a Lifetime of Clutter by Margareta Magnusson (Scribner)

How to Archive Family Keepsakes: Learn How to Preserve Family Photos, Memorabilia and Genealogy Records by Denise May Levenick (Family Tree Books)

How to Archive Family Photos: A Step-by-Step Guide to Organize and Share Your Photos Digitally by Denise May Levenick (Family Tree Books)

Keep the Memories, Lose the Stuff: Declutter, Downsize, and Move Forward with Your Life by Matt Paxton (Portfolio)

The Life-Changing Magic of Tidying Up: The Japanese Art of Decluttering and Organizing by Marie Kondō (Ten Speed Press)

Organize Your Genealogy: Strategies and Solutions for Every Researcher by Drew Smith (Family Tree Books)

Saving Stuff: How to Care for and Preserve Your Collectibles, Heirlooms, and Other Prized Possessions by Don Williams (Touchstone)

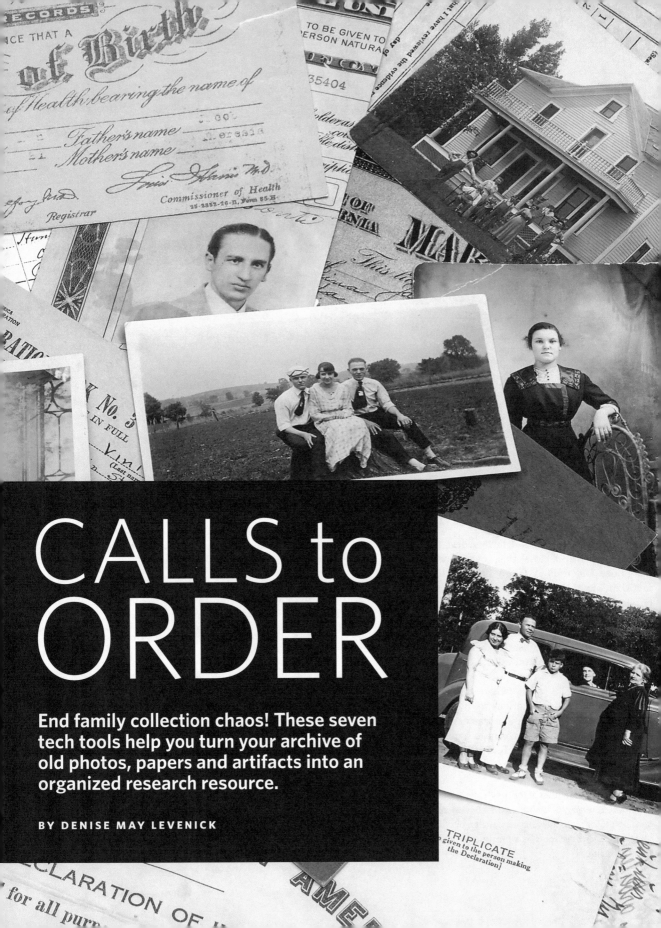

CALLS to ORDER

End family collection chaos! These seven tech tools help you turn your archive of old photos, papers and artifacts into an organized research resource.

BY DENISE MAY LEVENICK

At a Glance: Tech Tools to Organize Your Family Archive

TOOL	BEST USE	COST	KEY FEATURES	DRAWBACKS
Word processing software	Use Word or Google Docs to create a container inventory sheet for each box or album in your family archive.	Comes with most desktop computers. Google Docs is free with a Google account.	■ easy to use ■ Google Docs are accessible in your Google Drive	tables are simple, with limited flexibility in formatting and sorting
Spreadsheet software	Use Excel or Google Sheets to create a spreadsheet with details on each item in your archive.	Comes with most desktop computers. Google Sheets is free with a Google account.	■ flexible ■ powerful data sorting ■ Google Sheets are accessible in your Google Drive	spreadsheets can be cumbersome to use and navigate
Airtable <airtable.com>	Use this web-based software and mobile app for iOS and Android to create a family archive database synced on all your devices.	■ free basic version (up to 1,000 records and 1GB attachment space per "base") ■ subscriptions start at $20/month	■ free collaboration ■ access and edit on your mobile device ■ export to CSV file	limited exporting and printing options
Evernote <evernote.com>	Use this web-based software and app to create notes for items in your archive and organize them into notebooks.	■ free basic version is suitable for most family archives ■ subscriptions start at $14.99/month	■ compatible with most operating systems and devices ■ highly flexible ■ access and add notes on mobile device	limited exporting and printing options; free users can only use two devices
Recollector <maprecord.com/ recollector.html>	Use this desktop software to catalog your family archive.	$49	■ customizeable templates ■ share and sync via Dropbox ■ view data on free app ■ strong support	no online editing
Kindex <app.kindex.org>	Use this cloud-based software to catalog and transcribe your family archive, with record tags and captions (works best with Chrome or Safari).	■ free to participate in a project created by other users ■ 5/month for unlimited records ■ $10/month for unlimited records and collaboration features	■ access from your mobile device ■ export to CSV, XML, XIP ■ collaborate with relatives ■ designate an executor for your archive	data fields can't be customized
QromaScan and QromaTag <qroma.net>	Use these apps to digitize your photos and caption them with your voice.	QromaScan is free, though a $50 LightBox is recommended; QromaTag costs $4.99	■ automatically detects and applies tags when you speak about an image ■ sync tagged images via Dropbox	apps are iOS and/or Mac only

When you tag a digital photo with a name, place or subject, it becomes part of the metadata for that photo. What's metadata? It's information about a file, such as the format (for example, .PDF or .JPG), file size, date it was created and last opened, and for a photo, what camera or other capture device was used. And depending on that device, metadata might include the location of the image (also known as geotagging), camera settings and more.

So you might think of metadata as a caption that's automatically created. Unlike a photo caption, though, metadata is embedded within an image file and travels with the file. Two types of photo metadata are common today: EXIF data and IPTC data. You can customize IPTC data to include descriptive fields such as a caption or names.

Think of a photo tag as an index field, similar to those old subject titles in the library card catalog. You might tag a photo of your parents' first car with words like *car, automobile, Ford, sedan, 1969*. Add as many tags as makes sense. When you search your digitized photo storage system for the car tag, any image with that tag comes up. Therefore, it helps to use common words instead of trendy nicknames, and to create a master list of tags you're using.

Learn more about adding metadata and tagging photos and files in *How to Archive Family Photos* by Denise May Levenick (Family Tree Books).

tion of family heirlooms. She snaps a photo of each item with the Evernote app on her mobile phone, then enters a description with the names of relevant people, occasions and places. A tag such as *#diningroom* or *#office* indicates the location of the artifact.

Premium versions of Evernote will index any PDF files you attach to your notes—even brand names on objects like dishes. To take advantage of the text-recognition feature, photograph all sides of items like china or silver, which may have manufacturer and pattern or model details on the back.

You also can also create a simple, dedicated Table of Contents for all the notes in your Family Archive notebook.

5 Recollector

Recollector <www.collectingcatalog.com> is cross-platform management system designed for home collectors. Originally developed by an antique map enthusiast, the $49 software can be used to manage collections of any size and kind—including the photos, letters and artifacts in a typical family archive. It uses free mobile apps for Android and Apple iPhone and iPad to sync data via Dropbox and view your catalog from a library or family reunion. You can download a free trial version, which comes with a small collection catalog for users to work with.

You can view your collection data as a list, in an image gallery, or in a detailed single-item viewing window. Open images for high-resolution viewing. All fields are customizable. Recollector can be used as a general box inventory for a family archive, but it is ideal as a total family archive catalog.

Start a new collection catalog using the wizard from one of the software's included templates for different types of collections, or import data from a CSV file or Excel spreadsheet. The ready-to-go templates are set up for collections including art, books and photographs (great if you have a lot of photos), or choose the "generic" template and customize the fields. Another plus for family archivists is Recollector's new collaboration feature, which lets you share access to a collection file stored on Dropbox. Multiple users can input data, add images and view the collection. You'll appreciate the helpful training videos and comprehensive user guide. Frequent program updates and tutorials provide support for new and veteran Recollector users.

6 Kindex

Most family historians want to do more than simply preserve family photos and artifacts. We want to look into our ancestors' eyes in old photos or read between handwritten lines in their letters and journals. We want to share their stories with our family.

Cousins Kimball Clark and Cathy Gilmore created Kindex <app.kindex.org> when they needed a solution for managing their grandparents' family archive of letters, journals, photos and papers. Kindex web-based software, an Innovator Showdown award-winner at FamilySearch's 2017 RootsTec

TIP: Information you'll want to record about an heirloom includes what the item is, when it was created, who has owned it previously, what condition it's in, and where it's located now.

conference <rootstech.org>, offers private, searchable archives for collaboration, tagging, indexing and transcribing. A free online account allows users to start working immediately on a family archiving project. If you have a family tree on FamilySearch, you can add memories directly from your account. A $10-per-month subscription lets you catalog unlimited records in collaboration with relatives. And you can take the important step of designating an executor for your archive, should you ever become unable to manage it.

The software is ideal for a transcription project such as a diary or collection of letters. Decoding old handwriting can be time-consuming, but inviting help from family members leverages the power of crowdsourcing. Just upload digitized page images, transcribe the text, and then tag the record with names, places, dates and topics addressed in the document. Remember that transcriptions should be an exact copy of whatever is written, but your tags serve as a consistent vocabulary that makes retrieving the record easy. For example, your great-grandma might have called her oldest son Bob in one letter and Junior in another, but you'll give both letters a people tag of Robert Smith.

Kindex uses standard archival data fields, which you can see on the FAQ page <kindexblog.org/features>. You can export your archive records as an XLS (Microsoft Excel spreadsheet), CSV (comma-separated value), or a ZIP (compressed) file as a backup or to use in other software applications.

To get started, register for a free Kindex account and explore the Getting Started link <indexblog.org/getting-started-for-kindexers>.

Qroma

You might find it easier to just talk about a photo or artifact. Qroma (pronounced *crow-ma*) <qroma.net>, another 2017 Rootstech award-winner, automatically turns your words into captions and image file tags.

Its free QromaScan and QromaTag iPhone apps harness the power of mobile digital scanning and natural language-tagging technology to create an accurate, easy-to-use photo-identification system. You can start with existing photos from your phone's camera roll or a synced iCloud folder, or you can digitize photos, slides and negatives with the QromaScan app on your iPhone.

Two pieces of equipment improve the quality of your "scans" with optimized focus, lighting and camera angle: the QromaScan LightBox (about $50) for photos, and the SlideBox ($40) for 35 mm film and slides. Both boxes are foldable, portable and designed to work with your iPhone. They're optional, although some type of illuminating device is necessary when digitizing slides and negatives.

Now your images are ready for tagging. The QromaTag app hears "This is a photo of Hazel Harper Schuler taken in Pasadena at the Crandall Photo Studio," extracts the people, places and dates, and creates tags. These tags are stored in the metadata for the image file. QromaTag also transcribes the full text of your speech into the software's Description field, and places the name, place and date into the corresponding fields.

You can sync the tagged photos to your computer using Dropbox. Then when you view the image, you can see the metadata in the file Properties (Windows) or Get Info (Mac). According to the manufacturer, nearly every major operating system and most photo storage programs, such as Apple Photos and Adobe LightRoom, will index and use the metadata.

Actions within the apps are performed by touch or voice command. "Capture" scans the photo; "Template Off" allows the app to auto-detect the photograph size for scanning. Speak naturally, but clearly and firmly to enable voice recognition. Speak "People" to add a name directly to the People field. ∎

DENISE MAY LEVENICK is the Family Curator blogger <thefamilycurator.com> and author of *How to Archive Family Keepsakes* (Family Tree Books).

MORE ONLINE

@ **Web Content**

- 21 genealogy apps for research on-the-go <familytreemagazine.com/resources/apps/family-tree-apps>
- Family photo projects <familytreemagazine.com/projects/crafts/fun-family-photo-projects>
- How to digitize heirloom diaries and letters <familytreemagazine.com/premium/digitize-family-books-and-heirlooms>
- Create a table of contents note in Evernote <familytreemagazine.com/resources/apps/evernote-table-of-contents>
- Organize your family photos <familytreemagazine.com/organization/organizing-and-preserving-digital-photos>

Online Tree or Genealogy Software: Where to Keep Your Data

BY RICK CRUME

<www.familytreemagazine.com/resources/software/online-tree-vs-genealogy-software/>

Editor's note: Features and pricing information mentioned in this article were accurate as of December 2021, but may have changed. Please consult individual software providers for updated pricing.

Genealogy researchers need tools for recording names, dates, places, relationships, sources, family stories and photos. You might want to mine records and family trees on genealogy websites, and share your family history online. In the past, the most robust option for these tasks was traditional desktop software. Sure, online trees were great for finding cousins and getting record hints, but software offered the best tools for recording information on your ancestors, documenting sources and creating charts.

But technology has blurred the line between desktop programs and online trees. Software now embraces online features such as automated searching and syncing with websites, and online trees are more robust with attached media, record sources and more. Nowadays, you might find that a combination of the two methods—or even an online tree alone—best suits your needs.

To make an informed decision on what option is best for you, you'll need to know the basics on the best family history software and online family trees. In this article, we'll go over your tree-keeping options and help you choose what's right for you.

Either genealogy software or an online tree can help you accomplish essential research tasks, and a combo of the two adds flexibility. Consider the benefits of each option.

OPTION 1: GENEALOGY SOFTWARE

Genealogy software lets you record names, dates, places and relationships and add photos, records and stories. You can navigate around your family tree, cite your sources and create reports and wall charts to print or share as PDF files. Most of these programs are inexpensive and don't require any ongoing fees, except for optional upgrades. Your files reside on your hard drive, where you have complete control over them.

The most popular programs have been around for years and include many features and friendly user interfaces. Use this comparison chart to help you pick the best family tree software for you.

Now, almost all genealogy software offers online features. Most programs automatically search genealogy websites such as FamilySearch and give you hints to records or family trees that may match your ancestors.

Genealogy software can also automate your research on an ancestor by filling in search forms on genealogy websites with a single click. Hints usually cover only certain databases on a website, so you'll still want to experiment with different search criteria and search specific databases, but these features can save you a lot of time.

Most genealogy software can create reports for you to put on your own website, where they'll be easily accessible to anyone. Or, you can publish your family tree on a large genealogy site like Ancestry or MyHeritage. That's a lot easier than creating your own website, but you might have to pay a fee and your online family tree might be accessible only to other paying members and to people you invite.

Option 1: Desktop Genealogy Software, Compared

Name	Manufacturer	Cost	Mac?	Windows?	Mobile app?	Syncs with	Hints from
Ancestral Quest 16 <www.ancquest.com/index.htm>	Incline Software	$34.95 (Windows); $44.95 for Mac; (upgrade, $24.95 for Windows, $29.95 for Mac); Basics version, free	Yes	Yes	No	FamilySearch Family Tree	FamilySearch, Findmypast
Family Historian 7 <www.family-historian.co.uk>	Calico Pie Ltd	$64.95	No	Yes	No	n/a	Findmypast, MyHeritage
Family Tree Builder <www.familytreebuilder.com/family-tree-builder>	MyHeritage	free	Yes	Yes	Yes, MyHeritage for iOS and Android (free)	MyHeritage	FamilySearch, Geni, MyHeritage, WikiTree & others
Family Tree Maker 2019 <www.mackiev.com/ftm>	Software MacKiev	$79.95; (upgrade, $59.95)	Yes	Yes	Yes, for iOS and Android (free; no editing)	Ancestry	Ancestry, FamilySearch
Legacy Family Tree 9 <legacyfamilytree.com>	MyHeritage	$34.95 Deluxe Edition; (upgrade, $26.95)	No	Yes	Yes, Families for iOS and Android ($14.99)	FamilySearch Family Tree	FamilySearch, Findmypast, GenealogyBank, MyHeritage
Reunion 13 <www.leisterpro.com>	Leister Productions	$99; (upgrade, $49.95)	Yes	No	Yes, ReunionTouch for iOS ($9.99)	n/a	n/a
RootsMagic 8 <www.rootsmagic.com>	RootsMagic	$39.95 (upgrade, $29.95); Essentials version, free	Yes	Yes	Yes, for iOS and Android (free; no editing)	Ancestry, FamilySearch Family Tree	Ancestry, FamilySearch, Findmypast, MyHeritage

OPTION 2: ONLINE TREE(S)

Online family tree sites fall into two broad categories: On some, everybody has their own tree, while on others, everybody works together on a collaborative tree.

On sites like Ancestry and MyHeritage, each user has a separate tree and there's a lot of duplication between the trees. You can usually build a tree from scratch or start it with a GEDCOM file generated from your genealogy software or another online tree. You may be able to make your tree public or private and, either way, invite relatives to collaborate on it with you. If you have a public family tree, keep in mind that other users might copy your data, family photos and record images and add them to their own family trees without consulting with you first.

On FamilySearch, Geni (owned by MyHeritage), WeRelate and WikiTree, users collaborate on a unified tree and merge duplicates. Other users might make changes to profiles that you have added.

Online trees offer several advantages over traditional software: You never have to pay for a software update. You can access your tree from any computer or mobile device, and you don't have to worry about backing it up.

Our favorite family tree sites (see the chart below and on the next page) give you record hints and one-click searching on genealogy websites (though you should still do separate searches with different combinations of terms to get the most comprehensive matches). Some sites even create source citations and automatically attach record images. Ancestry Member Trees and the FamilySearch Family Tree have by far the best systems for maintaining an online family tree.

Protecting the privacy of living people is a key issue when you put your family tree online. Only the tree owner and anyone authorized by the owner can see living people in an Ancestry Member Tree. People without death information and born fewer than 125 years ago are considered to be living. In the FamilySearch Family Tree, you can see information on a living person only if you created the record. A person with no death information and who was born 110 or fewer years ago, married 95 or fewer years ago or had a child born 95 or fewer years ago is considered living.

Option 2: Online Tree Sites, Compared

Website	Cost	Mobile app?	Syncs with software?	Hints from
American Ancestors AncesTREES <www.americanancestors.org/tools/american-ancestrees>	2 GB of media storage, free; 10 GB, $19.95/year; 100 GB, DNA tools and private trees, $34.95; membership required to access most records ($34.95/3 months, $94.95/year)	n/a	n/a	American Ancestors, FamilySearch, Findmypast, & others
Ancestry.com <www.ancestry.com>	free trees; records: US ($24.99/month or $99/6 months; World ($39.99/month or $149/6-month; All-Access ($49.99/month, $199/6 months)	Yes, iOS and Android (free)	Family Tree Maker 2019, RootsMagic 8	Ancestry.com
FamilySearch Family Tree <www.familysearch.org>	free	Yes, two: Family-Search Tree and FamilySearch Memories; both iOS and Android (free)	Ancestral Quest 16, Legacy Family Tree 9, RootsMagic 8	FamilySearch
Findmypast <www.findmypast.com>	free trees; records: Essential British and Irish ($14.95/month or $129/year); Ultimate British and Irish ($19.95/month or $179/year)	Yes, for iOS and Android (free)	n/a	Findmypast

Option 2: Online Tree Sites, Compared (continued)

Website	Cost	Mobile app?	Syncs with software?	Hints from
Geneanet <en.geneanet.org>	tree with up to 1 GB of media storage, free; tree with up to 10 GB of media storage, plus advanced search options, $12.50/3 months	n/a	n/a	Geneanet
Genes Reunited <www.genesreunited.co.uk>	free trees; credits or subscription required for records access (see <www.genesreunited.co.uk/payments/subscription>)	n/a	n/a	Genes Reunited
Geni <www.geni.com>	free basic tree, $119.40 annual Pro subscription adds features	World Family Tree by TelGen, IOS and Android, ($6.99, no editing capabilities)	n/a	MyHeritage
MyHeritage <www.myheritage.com>	free basic tree; annual Premium ($129) or Premium Plus ($209) subscription required for larger trees; Data subscription ($129, first year; $189/year thereafter); Complete ($199, first year; $299/year thereafter)	MyHeritage, iOS and Android (free)	Family Tree Builder	FamilySearch, Geni, MyHeritage, WikiTree & others
RootsFinder <www.rootsfinder.com>	free, up to 2 GB media storage; $34.95/year, up to 100 GB media storage	n/a	n/a	American Ancestors, FamilySearch, Findmypast, Geni, MyHeritage, WikiTree & others
Tribal Pages <www.tribalpages.com>	tree with up to 50 photos, free; tree matching and up to 1000 photos, $36/year; tree matching and up to 10,000 photos, $48/year	n/a	n/a	n/a
WeRelate <www.werelate.org/wiki/Main_Page>	free	n/a	n/a	MyHeritage
WikiTree <www.wikitree.com>	free	n/a	n/a	n/a

OPTION 3: SOFTWARE-TREE COMBO

While the general trend in genealogy land is away from software and toward online trees and mobile apps, a combination of them still gives you the most flexibility.

For one thing, software helps you keep multiple online trees up to date. Many genealogists put their family tree on several websites to take advantage of hints from the sites' databases, and to connect with other researchers interested in those families.

It's worthwhile to have your family tree on any site where you've had a DNA test, so you and your matches can see how you're related. (You can upload a GEDCOM file to Ancestry, MyHeritage, FamilyTreeDNA and GEDmatch. Both Ancestry and MyHeritage also have robust tools to build an online tree.)

You might want to put your family tree on sites with connections to nationalities you're researching. Findmypast and Genes Reunited, for example, have strong British and Irish collections.

Finally, having your tree on a site with a mobile app lets you access it on your phone or tablet.

Option 3: Which Software and Trees Are Compatible

	Ancestry Member Trees	FamilySearch Family Tree	MyHeritage Trees
Ancestral Quest 16		Yes	
Family Tree Builder			Yes
Family Tree Maker 2019	Yes		
Legacy Family Tree 9		Yes	
RootsMagic 8	Yes	Yes	

What Syncs with What?

How do you keep your family tree up-to-date on all those sites and devices? Several programs now let you synchronize ("sync") the family file on your computer with trees online and on mobile devices. That copies not just names, dates and places, but also photos and record images, so everything is up-to-date on every device you use.

The chart above notes which sites each software syncs with:

- If you use MyHeritage, you can use the Family Tree Builder software on your computer and sync it with your trees on the MyHeritage site and the MyHeritage App.
- Both Family Tree Maker and RootsMagic synchronize with Ancestry Member Trees. But an Ancestry Member Tree can't handle to-do lists or research logs, so they aren't copied to your Ancestry Member Tree.
- Three software programs—Ancestral Quest, Legacy Family Tree and RootsMagic—sync with the FamilySearch Family Tree.

Syncing software with an online tree offers another advantage: If you ever let your subscription to Ancestry.com or MyHeritage lapse, you might lose access to the site's historical records that you attached to your tree. (Records uploaded from your computer will still be accessible.) If you've synchronized your trees, you'll still have access to all the records on your computer.

No single software syncs with every family tree website. To make it easier to update them all, you might keep a master file in one desktop program, such as Family Tree Maker, Legacy Family Tree or RootsMagic. Then sync the software with whatever websites you can. Whenever you've made significant updates to your software master file, export a GEDCOM to replace your tree on non-syncing sites. Keep in mind that a GEDCOM file includes only links to attached media files such as photos and document images; it doesn't include the media files themselves.

HOW TO CHOOSE THE RIGHT OPTION FOR YOU

To help you choose which platforms are right for your research needs, we've listed details such as the main features of each option, its strengths and drawbacks, the cost (if any), and what it syncs with. Then it will be up to you to decide which option best fits your current genealogy goals, and how you'd like to continue building your tree in the future. ●

Ancestry Member Trees

- **Host website:** Ancestry.com
- **Works best on:** the most current versions of Google Chrome (desktop and mobile), Mozilla Firefox (desktop) and Apple Safari (mobile)
- **Cost:** Registered guests can create, edit and share family trees for free. They can also respond to messages from other members and access free records, but viewing most records requires a subscription (US: $24.99/month or $99/6-month. World $39.99/month or $149/6-month. All-Access $49.99/month, $199/6-month)
- **Try it first:** Cancel a new subscription within 14 days and you won't be billed.
- **Mobile app:** Ancestry for iOS and Android
- **Syncs with:** Family Tree Maker and RootsMagic software
- **Main features:** Hints from Ancestry.com records and family trees. Easily add information from Ancestry.com to your tree. Connect with Ancestry Members researching the same families. Make your tree public, private and searchable (so people in your tree are found in searches), or private and not searchable. Link your tree to your AncestryDNA test.
- **Strengths:** Easy to use. Hints consolidate duplication in Member Tree matches. Sources are visually linked to the facts they support.
- **Drawbacks:** No family group sheets or pedigree charts. Access to "public" trees still requires an Ancestry.com subscription or invitation from a tree owner. Because it's easy to copy information from a tree, that results in massive duplication with dozens or more copies of the same profiles and trees. That makes it hard to find differences between the trees and to determine where the information originated.
- **Best for:** All users

Family Tree Maker 2019

- **Manufacturer:** Software MacKiev
- **Works best on:** Macintosh OS X 10.10 or later, Windows 7 or later
- **Cost:** $79.95 download, $59.95 upgrade
- **Try it first:** Free trial not available
- **Mobile app:** Family Tree Maker Connect for iOS and Android (free; no editing capabilities)
- **Syncs with:** Ancestry.com trees
- **Main features:** Build your family tree with attached photos and documents. Create charts, reports, timelines and interactive maps. Get hints to records on Ancestry.com and FamilySearch and search those sites from within the program. Synchronize your tree with an Ancestry Member Tree. Download an entire branch from a FamilySearch Family Tree into your Family Tree Maker file. Restore faded photos and color-code people in your tree.
- **Strengths:** You can copy and paste facts, along with related source citations, media items and notes, from one person to another. Source templates are organized by group and category. Choose from many attractive chart options. Easily publish your family tree on Ancestry.com, where it's accessible to subscribers and people you invite. FTM 2019 keeps track of your last thousand changes, so you can undo mistakes. With TreeVault, the program creates an online backup of your tree and lets you view the latest version of your tree on your smartphone or tablet.
- **Drawbacks:** More expensive than other programs, but still a good buy
- **Best for:** All users (and Ancestry.com users, in particular)

FamilySearch Family Tree

- **Host website:** FamilySearch
- **Works best on:** recent versions of most popular web browsers
- **Cost:** Free
- **Mobile app:** FamilySearch Tree and FamilySearch Memories, both for iOS and Android
- **Syncs with:** Ancestral Quest, Legacy Family Tree and RootsMagic software
- **Main features:** This collaborative family tree aims to avoid duplication and have just one profile for each person. Get hints from FamilySearch records. Search Ancestry.com, FamilySearch, Findmypast, MyHeritage and other sites. It has an excellent system for displaying photos, labeling them, organizing them in albums and sharing a link to an album with relatives.
- **Strengths:** The FamilySearch Family Tree is easy to use and an ideal way to preserve your family history for posterity. If you have an account and you're in the tree, the View My Relationship link shows how you're related to someone else in the tree. Use a person's Discussions area under the Collaborate tab to share comments with other researchers.
- **Drawbacks:** Instead of helping you create complete source citations, the site just asks you to provide the "reason this information is correct." You might feel uncomfortable using a collaborative tree, in which other researchers can change your ancestors' profiles, as your only tree.
- **Best for:** All users, especially as a second tree.

Findmypast

- **Host website:** Findmypast
- **Works best on:** Recent versions of all major web browsers
- **Cost:** You can build your online tree for free and attach some Findmypast records, including US census records, for free. Access to other records requires a subscription. Findmypast offers two subscriptions: Essential British and Irish ($14.95/month or $129/12 months) or Ultimate British and Irish ($19.95/month or $179/12 months). Alternatively, you can pay as you go by purchasing "credits" that are valid for a certain period of time.
- **Try it first:** Free 14-day trial
- **Mobile app:** Yes, for Android and iOS
- **Syncs with:** Not available
- **Main features:** This UK-based genealogy site focuses on UK and Irish records, including newspapers, Irish Roman Catholic parish records, and the National Burial Index for England and Wales. It also has large US and Canadian collections, including marriages, the census, and the Periodical Source Index (PERSI) to articles in genealogy and history magazines. Online trees here get hints to Findmypast records.
- **Strengths:** Large British and Irish record collections. Automated record hints.
- **Drawbacks:** No charts and reports.
- **Best for:** Using as a second tree, especially for Findmypast subscribers

Legacy Family Tree 9.0

- **Manufacturer:** MyHeritage
- **Works best on:** Windows 7 or higher
- **Cost:** $34.95 download; $26.95 upgrade
- **Try it first:** free Standard Edition
- **Mobile app:** Families, $14.99, by TelGen Ltd.
- **Syncs with:** FamilySearch; version 10 is expected to sync with MyHeritage
- **Main features:** Enable hints to get them from FamilySearch, Findmypast, GenealogyBank and MyHeritage. Search Ancestry.com, FamilySearch, Find a Grave, Findmypast, GenealogyBank, MyHeritage, Newspapers.com and other sites from within the program. Display up to seven views of the same family file or two different family files at the same time, and drag and drop people between files. It's easy to find and merge duplicate people. Choose from many charting options and use powerful tools to search for people in your file.
- **Strengths:** Excellent reports, including reports for your website. Print reports in multiple languages.
- **Drawbacks:** The screen is cluttered and the clipboard tool for adding sources uses unintuitive icons.
- **Best for:** Users who want to create a well-documented family history and create outstanding reports.

MyHeritage/Family Tree Builder

- **Manufacturer and host website:** MyHeritage
- **Works best on:** Windows XP and later, or Mac OS X
- **Cost:** It's free to download Family Tree Builder software and build basic trees (an unlimited offline family file plus up to 250 people on MyHeritage). To build larger trees on MyHeritage and view many Record Matches, you'll need a MyHeritage subscription (Premium with up to 2,500 people: $129/year (first year, $89); Premium Plus with unlimited tree and enhanced Smart Matching: $209/year (first year, $149); Data with access to MyHeritage premium records and Record Matches: $189/year (first year, $129); Complete Plan of PremiumPlus and Data: $299/year (first year, $199)
- **Try it first:** Download Family Tree Builder for free.
- **Mobile app:** MyHeritage for iOS and Android
- **Syncs with:** MyHeritage.com
- **Main features:** Make your online tree public or limit access to MyHeritage members you invite; optionally, let family members edit it. Get hints from MyHeritage records and trees. Search MyHeritage record collections and record test results from MyHeritage DNA.
- **Strengths:** You can mark people, facts and notes as private in your Family Tree Builder file, so they don't synchronize to your online tree. Family Tree Builder software and the MyHeritage site is available in more than 40 languages.
- **Drawbacks:** The online tree and Family Tree Builder offer a no-frills source documentation system.
- **Best for:** Users who want hints to records and family trees from around the world.

RootsMagic 8

- **Manufacturer:** RootsMagic
- **Works best on:** Windows 7 SP1 and above or Mac OS 10.12 and above
- **Cost:** $39.95 download, $29.95 upgrade
- **Try it first:** The free RootsMagic Essentials includes the full version's core features.
- **Mobile app:** RootsMagic App for iOS and Android lets you view (but not edit) your RootsMagic files, and convert files from other genealogy software to RootsMagic files.
- **Syncs with:** Ancestry.com, FamilySearch
- **Main features:** The latest version offers a more modern, streamlined look with simpler navigation, easier editing, reusable source citations, fan charts and native support for MacOS. You can create many colorful reports and wallcharts. Publish your family tree and pictures on your own private website with the free My RootsMagic hosting service.
- **Strengths:** Once you match a person in your RootsMagic file with someone in the FamilySearch Family Tree, you can copy information back and forth between those profiles. A feature called TreeShare lets you synchronize the RootsMagic file on your computer with your Ancestry Member Tree online.
- **Drawbacks:** Unlike the FamilySearch Family Tree, RootsMagic and other programs can't display an album with large thumbnails of all of a person's pictures.
- **Best for:** All users, especially those who have family trees on both Ancestry and FamilySearch.

A version of this article originally appeared in the October/November 2017 issue of *Family Tree Magazine*. Last updated, December 2021.

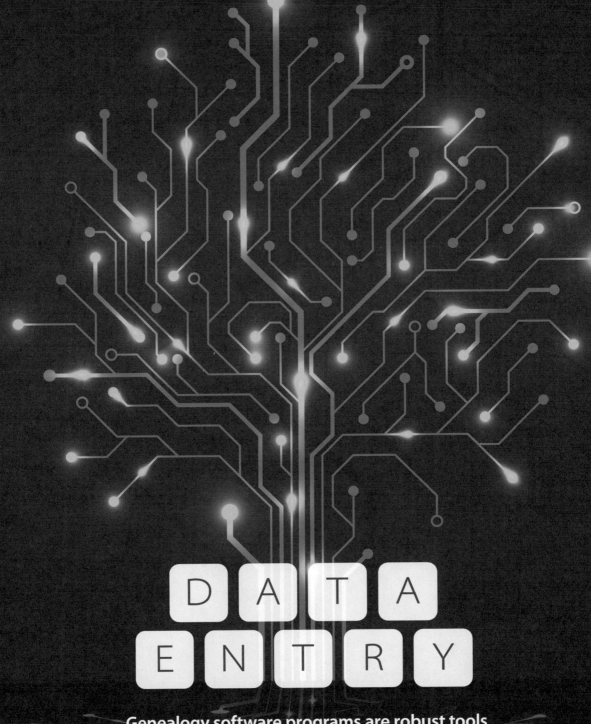

DATA ENTRY

Genealogy software programs are robust tools for building your family tree. Here's how to best add key facts to them: names, dates and places.

At a basic level, it's easy to enter names, dates and places in genealogy software. But how should you record name changes, approximate dates, and places that no longer exist? Genealogy software can handle just about any variations—if you know where they should go and how to enter them.

Here are some power-user tips for entering data into your genealogy software, regardless of what program you're using. Throughout, we'll use the most-popular programs (Ancestral Quest <www.ancquest.com>, Family Tree Builder <www.myheritage.com/family-tree-builder>, Family Tree Maker <www.mackiev.com/ftm>, Legacy Family Tree <www.legacyfamilytree.com> and RootsMagic <www.rootsmagic.com>) as examples.

ENTERING NAMES

Most genealogy software has a field for Given (first) Names and another one for Surname (last name). But it's not always as simple as entering *John* in the former and *Smith* in the latter. You might also want to record titles, nicknames, alternate spellings and name changes, plus surnames made up of multiple words.

Keep these points in mind when entering people's names in your genealogy software.

Maiden names

Standard practice is to enter a woman's maiden name as her surname. Note that, in some programs, you'll need to run online records searches for a woman's maiden name as well as her married name; some don't automatically search for both.

Multiword surnames

Sometimes a surname is made up of more than one word, such as "von der Leyen" or "di Giovanni." Names from Hispanic cultures may combine the surnames of both parents, like "Vargas Llosa."

Enter all of a surname's words—whether just one or many—in the Surname field. In Family Tree Maker, click the Edit Name Parts button

to make sure words are populating the search fields correctly.

Titles

A prefix, such as *Capt.*, *Dr.* or *Rev.*, might precede a name and a suffix, such as *M.D.*, *Sr.* or *III* ("the third"), might follow it. All the popular genealogy programs have fields for Prefix or Title/Prefix, and Suffix or Title/Suffix.

Nicknames

Ancestral Quest, Family Tree Builder and Roots-Magic each have a field for Nickname. Family Tree Maker recommends entering a nickname in the Also Known As field, and Legacy Family Tree suggests that you enter a nickname as an Alternative Name.

Name variations

A person's name might be spelled multiple ways in different records (or even in the same record!). My ancestor John Robertson's name usually appears in census records as "John Robinson" or "John Robison." And I've found many variations of my relative John Hudson Pennington's name, including: "Col. J. H. Pennington," "J. Hudson Pennington" and even "Colonel Jeremiah H. Pennington." Your ancestor might have even changed his name altogether. My immigrant ancestor Johann Carl Schantz became "Charles Jones."

All the major programs have a way to indicate name variations. You can enter variants as an "AKA" in Ancestral Quest, an "Alias" in Family Tree Builder, an "Also Known As" in Family Tree Maker and an "Alternate Name" in Legacy Family Tree and RootsMagic. When entering an Alternate Name fact in RootsMagic, you can specify the name type (such as AKA, nickname, maiden name, or alternate spelling).

You might also create a separate fact (AKA, Also Known As, Alternative Name or Nickname) for each nickname and name variation. When you enter a name variation, add a note indicating where you found that version of the name.

East Asian names

Most popular genealogy software programs follow the European naming convention that places given names first and the surname last. But in some places, such as China, Japan and

Korea, the surname typically comes first. These names would display correctly if you entered surnames in the Given Names field and given names in the Surname field. But that's not a good long-term solution, and it's not recommended.

Unlike most genealogy programs, Ancestral Quest can display Asian names properly, both onscreen and in reports. To change the setting for everyone in your file, click on Tools > Preferences and, under the Database tab, select the option to set a default language template for the file. Change the template to Chinese, and surnames will appear first. To change the name order for just selected individuals in your Ancestral Quest file, go to each person's Edit Individual screen and select a different language template.

Users of other programs should enter East Asian given names and surnames in the appropriate fields, even though they won't display in the correct order.

Genealogy Software: Compared

Here are the most popular family tree-building software programs. All except Legacy Family Tree are available for both Windows and Mac, and all except Family Tree Maker offer free versions. (Legacy Family Tree will run, with some limitations, on a Mac that uses an emulator or other Windows operating system.)

For more detail (and a comparison with online family trees), see <www.familytreemagazine.com/resources/software/online-tree-vs-genealogy-software>.

Name	Price	Notes
Ancestral Quest 16 <www.ancquest.com>	$34.95	A good choice for long-time users of the defunct Personal Ancestral File (PAF) who want to stick with a similar user interface. Free "Basics" version available
Family Tree Builder <www.myheritage.com/family-tree-builder>	free	Automatically searches for matches on MyHeritage and FamilySearch, and can sync with MyHeritage family trees
Family Tree Maker 2019 <www.mackiev.com/ftm>	$79.95	Offers hints from Ancestry.com and FamilySearch and can sync with Ancestry.com family trees with a single click. Notable for its wide variety of charts and reports.
Legacy Family Tree 9.0 <www.legacyfamilytree.com>	$34.95	Offers record searching from FamilySearch, Find a Grave, Findmypast, GenealogyBank, MyHeritage. Free "Standard" edition available
RootsMagic 8 <www.rootsmagic.com>	$39.95	Easy editing and simple navigation. Offer hints from Ancestry.com, FamilySearch, Findmypast and MyHeritage. Share tree data back and forth with Ancestry.com and FamilySearch. Free "Essentials" version available

Genealogy software can handle just about any variations—
if you know where they should go and how to enter them.

GALEANU MIHAI /ISTOCK

ENTERING DATES

Most genealogy software displays dates as *DD Month YYYY* (e.g., *7 Nov 1960*) onscreen and in reports, since that format is compact and avoids confusion. Other constructions, such as the US standard of *MM/DD/YYYY*, could be misinterpreted (e.g., *11/7/1960* as *11 Jul 1960* instead of *7 Nov 1960*). If you prefer a different format, you can change your software's date setting.

If you don't have an exact date, you could enter a partial date, such as a year or month and year. You could also precede an uncertain date with a qualifier like *abt* (about), *bef* (before) or *aft* (after). Or, to indicate an event took place between two dates, you could enter it as *between 1 Jan 1900 and 5 Jan 1900*. You could do something similar for an event that took place over multiple dates: *from 1 Jan 1900 to 5 Jan 1900*.

ENTERING PLACES

Generally, you should organize a place name from the smallest to the largest jurisdiction, including every level. A complete US place name typically includes a town/township/city, plus the county, state and country: *Victoria, Knox, Illinois, United States.*

Counties and townships

The word *County* is usually omitted, but I like to include it if the county name is unclear or unknown. For example: *Becker, Minnesota, United States* could be interpreted as Becker County or the town of Becker (which is in a different county, Sherburne County). To avoid confusion, you could enter *Becker County, Minnesota, United States* for the county and *Becker, Sherburne, Minnesota, United States* for the town.

If the place is in a rural township, I include the word *Township*. That way, *Glyndon Township, Clay, Minnesota, United States* is distinct from *Glyndon, Clay, Minnesota, United States*, which refers to the separate town of Glyndon.

Cemeteries and churches

You can also record a specific place, such as a church or a cemetery. That can go in the Place Details field in RootsMagic. In Ancestral Quest 16 and Family Tree Maker 2019, you can enter a specific place like a church or a cemetery before the town in the place name. In Legacy Family

Tree, put it in the notes for the fact. (In the Individual's Information window, select the fact and click the Edit button). In Family Tree Builder, you can enter a specific place either before the town in the place name or in the Description field for the fact under the Facts tab.

Defunct place names

Many county, state and national boundaries have changed over time. You can enter the place name either as it was at the time of the event, or as it is known today. Just be consistent, and stick to one standard or the other.

If you enter a historical place name in the Place field, you could note the modern name in the Place Details or the Place Description field. For example, my grandfather was born in South Dakota before it reached statehood. I can enter *Enterprise Township, Moody County, Dakota Territory, United States* as his place of birth, but note in the Place Details or Description that it's now *Enterprise Township, Moody County, South Dakota, United States*. Likewise, I could enter the modern name in the Place field and note the place name at the time of his birth in the Place Details or Description.

When you enter a location, Family Tree Maker checks it against a database of more than 3 million modern, standardized place names (*not* historical ones). If the place is unrecognized, the box to the right turns into a question mark. Click on it to resolve the place name.

RootsMagic's CountyCheck feature alerts you if you enter a county that didn't exist at the date of the event. CountyCheck is on by default in Settings > Program Settings, and it covers counties in the United States, Canada, the United Kingdom and Australia.

HANDLING FOREIGN LANGUAGES

If there's a Jürgen, a Françoise, or another name with a diacritical mark in your family tree, you might want to take advantage of these tools for entering foreign-language characters like *ü* and *ç*.

Ancestral Quest: In the Edit Individual window, click on Tools > Character Map. Select one or more characters to copy and click the Copy button. Then go to a name or place and paste the character (Ctrl-V).

For more cross-platform advice on family tree-building programs, read <www.familytreemagazine.com/resources/software/top-10-genealogy-software-tricks>.

Family Tree Builder: To open the Windows Character Map, press the Windows key + R to open the Run command box, type *charmap* and press Enter. On a Mac, you can use macOS shortcuts.

Family Tree Maker: When you enter a person's name, click on the pencil icon to the right to open the Edit Name box. Then click where you want to enter the special character, and hit the Insert Symbol button.

Legacy Family Tree: In the Individual's Information window, place your cursor where you want to insert the special character, then press the F6 key. Double-click on one or more characters and hit Return Characters. You can also select up to eight special characters that you use most often and make them immediately accessible in the Special Characters ribbon to the left of the Events/Facts on every input window. Click on the blue box at the top of the ribbon. In the window that opens, double-click on up to eight characters and hit Return Characters. To insert a character, just click where you want to insert it and then on the special character in the ribbon.

RootsMagic: Right-click on any edit or note field and select Character Map. Choose a character set from the Subset drop-down, select a letter and click Insert. On a Mac, hold down the letter you wish to accent, such as "e." Wait a second and the Accent Menu will appear. Then click on the character you want to enter. The RootsMagic Wiki <wiki.rootsmagic.com/wiki/RootsMagic_8:Entering_International_Characters> also has advice for using Microsoft Word, Windows and macOS shortcuts to enter accented characters in RootsMagic.

Names, dates and places are core components of an accurate family history, so it's worthwhile to record them carefully. ●

Contributing Editor **Rick Crume** specializes in online research, genealogy software, DNA testing and British genealogy.

Made in the USA
Columbia, SC
15 March 2024

32741077R00059